S0-ADT-685

Complete Early Skills

Carson-Dellosa Publishing LLC
Greensboro, North Carolina

Carson-Dellosa Publishing LLC
P.O. Box 35665
Greensboro, NC 27425 USA

© 2011 Carson-Dellosa Publishing LLC. Except as permitted under the United States Copyright Act, no part of this publication may be reproduced, stored, or distributed in any form or by any means (mechanically, electronically, recording, etc.) without the prior written consent of Carson-Dellosa Publishing LLC.

Printed in the USA • All rights reserved.

ISBN 978-1-62399-096-1

03-364137811

Table of Contents

READING

Name _____

Name, Address, Phone

This book belongs to

- -

I live at

- -

The city I live in is

- -

The province or territory I live in is

- -

My phone number is

- -

Name _____

Review the Alphabet

Directions: Practise writing the letters.

Review the Alphabet

Directions: Practise writing the letters.

Name _____

Review the Alphabet

Directions: Practise writing the letters.

- -

- -

- -

- -

- -

- -

Name _____

Letter Recognition

Directions: In each set, match the lower-case letter to the upper-case letter.

a   C

f   H

c   J

h   E

e   A

j   F

g   D

b   B

i   M

d   G

k   I

l   L

m   K

Name _____

Letter Recognition

Directions: In each set, match the lower-case letter to the upper-case letter.

n   U

s   P

p   R

u   Q

r   N

q   S

t   V

y   O

v   T

o   W

x   Z

w   Y

z   X

Name _____

Beginning Consonants: Bb, Cc, Dd, Ff

Beginning consonants are the sounds that come at the beginning of words. Consonants are the letters b, c, d, f, g, h, j, k, l, m, n, p,q, r, s, t, v, w, x, y and z.

Directions: Say the name of each letter. Say the sound each letter makes. Circle the letters that make the beginning sound for each picture.

Bb   Cc   Dd   Ff

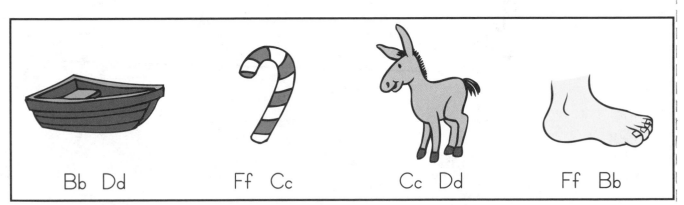

Bb Dd   Ff Cc   Cc Dd   Ff Bb

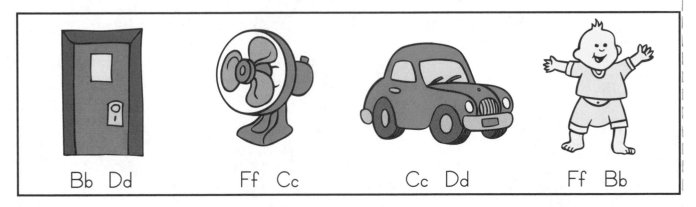

Bb Dd   Ff Cc   Cc Dd   Ff Bb

Name _____

Beginning Consonants: Bb, Cc, Dd, Ff

Directions: Say the name of each letter. Say the sound each letter makes. Draw a line from each letter to the picture which begins with that sound.

Ff

Dd

Cc

Bb

Dd

Ff

Cc

Bb

Name _____

Beginning Consonants: Gg, Hh, Jj, Kk

Directions: Say the name of each letter. Say the sound each letter makes. Trace the letter pair that makes the beginning sound in each picture.

Gg　　　Hh　　　Jj　　　Kk

Kk　　　Hh

Gg　　　Kk

Gg　　　Hh

Jj　　　Gg

Beginning Consonants: Gg, Hh, Jj, Kk

Directions: Say the name of each letter. Say the sound each letter makes. Draw a line from each letter pair to the picture which begins with that sound.

Gg

Kk

Hh

Jj

Kk

Hh

Jj

Gg

Name _____

Beginning Consonants: Ll, Mm, Nn, Pp

Directions: Say the name of each letter. Say the sound each letter makes. Trace the letters. Then draw a line from each letter pair to the picture which begins with that sound.

Ll Mm Nn Pp

Ll

Mm

Nn

Pp

Name _____

Beginning Consonants: Ll, Mm, Nn, Pp

Directions: Say the name of each letter. Say the sound each letter makes. Trace the letter pair that makes the beginning sound in each picture.

Ll   Mm   Nn   Pp

Mm   Ll

Mm   Pp

Ll   Nn

Pp   Mm

Name _____

Beginning Consonants: Qq, Rr, Ss, Tt

Directions: Say the name of each letter. Say the sound each letter makes. Trace the letter pair in the boxes. Then colour the picture which begins with that sound.

Qq   Rr   Ss   Tt

Name _____

Beginning Consonants: Qq, Rr, Ss, Tt

Directions: Say the name of each letter. Say the sound each letter makes. Draw a line from each letter pair to the picture which begins with that sound.

Qq

Ss

Rr

Tt

Tt

Ss

Rr

Qq

Name _____

Beginning Consonants: Vv, Ww, Xx, Yy, Zz

Directions: Say the name of each letter. Say the sound each letter makes. Trace the letters. Then draw a line from each letter pair to the picture which begins with that sound.

Vv   Ww   Xx   Yy   Zz

Name _____

Beginning Consonants: Vv, Ww, Xx, Yy, Zz

Directions: Say the name of each letter. Say the sound each letter makes. Then draw a line from each letter pair to the picture which begins with that sound.

Vv

Zz

Xx

Yy

Ww

Vv

Zz

Yy

Ww

Xx

Ending Consonants: b, d, f

Ending consonants are the sounds that come at the end of words.

Directions: Say the name of each picture. Then write the letter which makes the **ending** sound for each picture.

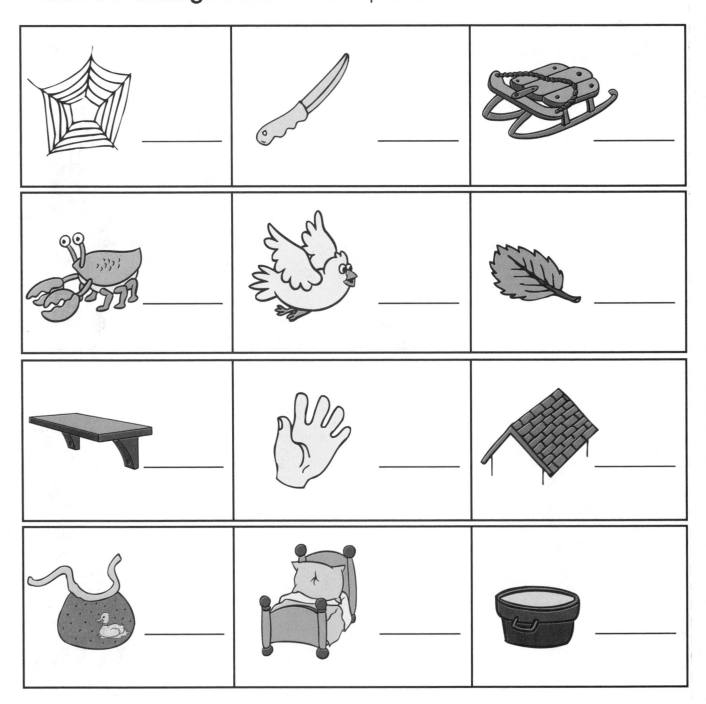

Name _____

Ending Consonants: g, m, n

Directions: Say the name of each picture. Draw a line from each letter to the pictures which end with that sound.

g

m

n

g

m

n

Name _____

Ending Consonants: k, l, p

Directions: Trace the letters in each row. Say the name of each picture. Then colour the pictures in each row which end with that sound.

k

l

p

Name _____

Ending Consonants: r, s, t, x

Directions: Say the name of each picture. Then circle the ending sound for each picture.

    r s t x

    r s t x

    r s t x

    r s t x

    r s t x

    r s t x

    r s t x

    r s t x

Short Vowels

Vowels are the letters **a**, **e**, **i**, **o** and **u**. Short **a** is the sound you hear in **ant**. Short **e** is the sound you hear in **elephant**. Short **i** is the sound you hear in **igloo**. Short **o** is the sound you hear in **octopus**. Short **u** is the sound you hear in **umbrella**.

Directions: Say the short vowel sound at the beginning of each row. Say the name of each picture. Then colour the pictures which have the same short vowel sounds as that letter.

Name _____

Short Vowel Sounds

Directions: In each box are three pictures. The words that name the pictures have missing letters. Write **a, e, i, o** or **u** to finish the words.

p ___ n

p ___ n

p ___ n

b ___ g

b ___ g

b ___ g

c ___ t

c ___ t

c ___ t

h ___ t

h ___ t

h ___ t

Long Vowels

Vowels are the letters **a**, **e**, **i**, **o** and **u**. Long vowel sounds say their own names. Long **a** is the sound you hear in **hay**. Long **e** is the sound you hear in **me**. Long **i** is the sound you hear in **pie**. Long **o** is the sound you hear in **no**. Long **u** is the sound you hear in **cute**.

Directions: Say the long vowel sound at the beginning of each row. Say the name of each picture. Colour the pictures in each row that have the same long vowel sound as that letter.

Name _____

Long Vowel Sounds

Directions: Write **a, e, i, o** or **u** in each blank to finish the word. Draw a line from the word to the picture.

c ___ ke

r ___ se

k ___ te

f ___ t

m ___ le

29

Words With a

Directions: Each train has a group of pictures. Write the word that names the pictures. Read your rhyming words.

These trains use the short **a** sound like in the word cat:

These trains use the long **a** sound like in the word lake:

Name _____

Short and Long Aa

Directions: Say the name of each picture. If it has the short **a** sound, colour it **red**. If it has the long **a** sound, colour it **yellow**.

 ă

 ā

Words With e

Directions: Short **e** sounds like the **e** in hen. Long **e** sounds like the **e** in bee. Look at the pictures. If the word has a short **e** sound, draw a line to the **hen** with your **red** crayon. If the word has a long **e** sound, draw a line to the **bee** with your **green** crayon.

hen　　　**bee**

Short and Long Ee

Directions: Say the name of each picture. Circle the pictures which have the short **e** sound. Draw a triangle around the pictures which have the long **e** sound.

ĕ

ē

Name _____

Words With i

Directions: Short **i** sounds like the **i** in pig. Long **i** sounds like the **i** in kite. Draw a circle around the words with the short **i** sound. Draw an **X** on the words with the long **i** sound.

pin

five

pig

slide

kite

lid

tie

bib

pie

GRADE 1

Name _____

Short and Long Ii

Directions: Say the name of each picture. If it has the short **i** sound, colour it **yellow**. If it has the long **i** sound, colour it **red**

ĭ

ī

GRADE 1

Name _____

Words With o

Directions: The short **o** sounds like the **o** in dog. Long **o** sounds like the **o** in rope. Draw a line from the picture to the word that names it. Draw a circle around the word if it has a short **o** sound.

hot dog

fox

blocks

rose

boat

Name _____

Short and Long Oo

Directions: Say the name of each picture. If the picture has the long **o** sound, write a **green L** on the blank. If the picture has the short **o** sound, write a **red S** on the blank.

_____

_____

_____

_____

_____

_____

_____

_____

Name _____

Words With u

Directions: The short **u** sounds like the **u** in bug. The long **u** sounds like the **u** in blue. Draw a circle around the words with short **u**. Draw an **X** on the words with long **u**.

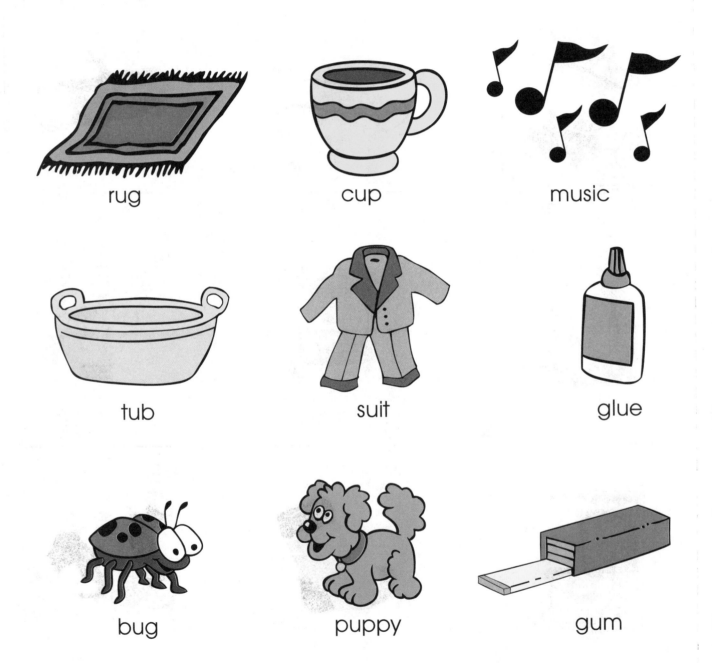

rug

cup

music

tub

suit

glue

bug

puppy

gum

Short and Long Uu

Directions: Say the name of each picture. If it has the long **u** sound, write a **u** in the **unicorn** column. If it has the short **u** sound, write a **u** in the **umbrella** column.

ū

ŭ

Super Silent E

When you add an **e** to the end of some words, the vowel changes from a short vowel sound to a long vowel sound. The **e** is silent.

Example: rip + **e** = ripe.

Directions: Say the word under the first picture in each pair. Then add an **e** to the word under the next picture. Say the new word.

pet   _____   tub   _____

man   _____   kit   _____

pin   _____   cap   _____

Consonant Blends

Consonant blends are two or more consonant sounds together in a word. The blend is made by combining the consonant sounds.

Example: **fl**oor

Directions: The name of each picture begins with a **blend**. Circle the beginning blend for each picture.

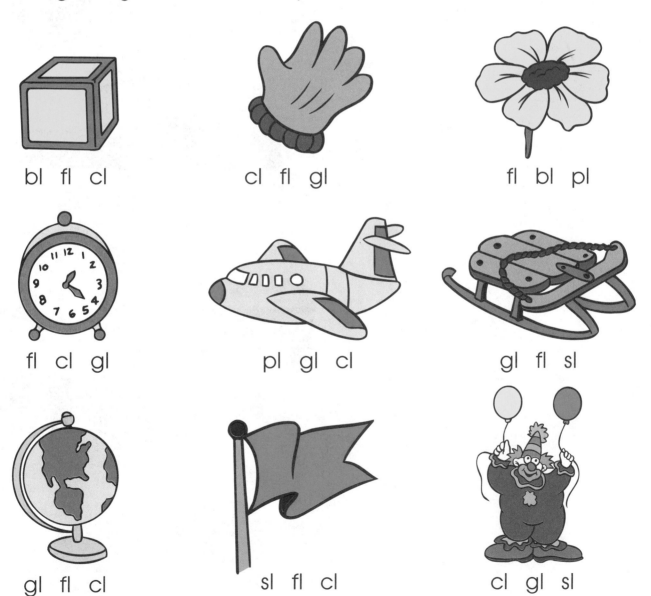

bl fl cl

cl fl gl

fl bl pl

fl cl gl

pl gl cl

gl fl sl

gl fl cl

sl fl cl

cl gl sl

Consonant Blends

Directions: The beginning blend for each word is missing. Fill in the correct blend to finish the word. Draw a line from the word to the picture.

_____ ain

_____ og

_____ ab

_____ um

_____ ush

_____ esent

Name _____

Consonant Blends

Directions: Draw a line from the picture to the blend that begins its word.

sk

sl

sm

sn

sp

st

sw

43

GRADE 1

Name _____

Consonant Blends

Directions: Look at the first picture in each row. Circle the pictures in the row that begin with the same sound.

chair

shell

thumb

wheel

Beginning Blends

Directions: Say the blend for each word as you search for it.

```
b   l   o   s   l   e   d   a   b   f   t   k   a   i   n
l   b   r   e   a   d   x   s   t   o   p   i   x   a   p
o   l   g   u   f   e   n   p   s   p   i   d   e   r   i
c   l   o   w   n   a   w   l   p   z   j   c   r   a   b
k   t   c   e   n   t   h   s   t   e   g   l   q   c   r
d   h   b   r   e   a   e   j   w   k   x   o   w   h   y
h   u   s   n   a   k   e   m   d   j   l   c   m   a   j
v   m   i   u   k   l   l   s   k   u   n   k   c   i   f
i   b   g   l   o   b   e   m   h   n   o   q   t   r   r
b   f   l   j   x   s   y   a   z   s   p   e   d   o   o
s   h   e   l   l   w   k   l   f   s   s   v   u   p   g
h   a   r   l   c   a   d   l   l   v   w   k   z   s   n
o   z   y   q   s   n   l   t   a   h   n   r   u   m   q
e   f   l   o   w   e   r   a   g   l   o   v   e   e   r
w   g   m   b   c   e   n   m   o   p   d   o   f   l   g
p   r   e   s   e   n   t   r   a   i   n   b   p   l   i
```

Words to find:

block	sled	globe	crab
clock	frog	present	flower
train	glove	skunk	snake
swan	flag	smell	spider
bread	small	chair	shell
stop	sled	shoe	
thumb	wheel	clown	

Ending Consonant Blends

Directions: Write **lt** or **ft** to complete the words.

be _____

ra _____

sa _____

qui _____

le _____

Name _____

Ending Consonant Blends

Directions: Draw a line from the picture to the blend that ends the word.

lf

lk

sk

st

Name _____

Ending Consonant Blends

Directions: Every juke box has a word ending and a list of letters. Add each of the letters to the word ending to make rhyming words.

___and

b _____
h _____
l _____
s _____

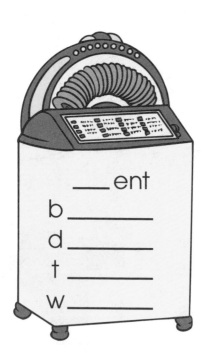

___ent

b _____
d _____
t _____
w _____

___ump

b _____
d _____
j _____
p _____

___ink

p _____
s _____
l _____
th_____

___ing

r _____
s _____
st _____
k _____

___ank

b _____
r _____
s _____
t _____

Name _____

Ending Consonant Blends

Directions: Say the blend for each word as you search for it.

```
b  e  l  t  l  e  m  m  i  l  k  r  p
b  r  l  z  m  a  a  i  u  v  r  i  n
r  r  d  u  m  p  s  h  n  x  i  t  a
i  b  p  i  n  g  k  p  i  b  n  g  w
n  m  k  i  q  i  w  e  n  t  g  d  s
g  t  h  i  n  k  n  c  e  s  i  r  h
e  e  i  k  i  f  h  r  c  d  x  e  e
t  c  s  j  b  c  l  a  s  p  n  m  l
e  r  i  e  l  o  m  n  i  y  e  p  f
n  b  n  b  a  n  d  k  g  o  s  f  k
t  a  g  l  n  a  l  a  n  d  t  e  d
x  d  c  o  k  u  z  j  e  l  u  m  p
r  a  f  t  b  r  h  s  h  r  i  n  k
```

Words to find:

belt	raft	milk	shelf
mask	clasp	nest	band
think	went	lump	crank
ring	blank	shrink	land
bring	tent	dump	sing

Name _____

Rhyming Words

Rhyming words are words that sound alike at the end of the word. **Cat** and **hat** rhyme.

Directions: Draw a circle around each word pair that rhymes. Draw an **X** on each pair that does not rhyme.

Example:

(soap rope)

red
dog

book
hook

cold
rock

cat
hat

yellow
black

one
two

rock
sock

rat
flat

good
nice

you
to

meet
toy

old
sold

sale
whale

word
letter

Name _____

Rhyming Words

Rhyming words are words that sound alike at the end of the word.

Directions: Draw a line to match the pictures that rhyme. Write two of your rhyming word pairs below.

ABC Order

Directions: Abc order is the order in which letters come in the alphabet. Draw a line to connect the dots. Follow the letters in **abc** order. Then colour the picture.

Name _____

ABC Order

Directions: Draw a line to connect the dots. Follow the letters in abc order. Then colour the picture.

Name _____

ABC Order

Directions: Circle the first letter of each word. Then put each pair of the words in abc order.

   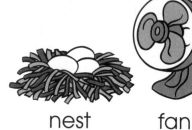

Ⓒar   Ⓑird   moon   two   nest   fan

bird

car

card   dog   pig   bike   sun   pie

Name _____

ABC Order

Directions: Look at the words in each box. Circle the word that comes first in abc order.

duck four rock	chair apple yellow	peach this walk
game boy pink	light come one	mouse ten orange
angel table hair	zebra watch five	foot boat mine
look blue rope	who dog black	book tan six

Name _____

Compound Words

Compound words are two words that are put together to make one new word.

Directions: Look at the pictures and the two words that are next to each other. Put the words together to make a new word. Write the new word.

Example:

 + =

house   boat

houseboat

 + =

side   walk

_____

 + =

lip   stick

_____

 + =

sand   box

_____

 + =

lunch   box

_____

Compound Words

Directions: Circle the compound word which completes each sentence. Write each word on the lines.

1. The _____ brings us letters.

        mailman   snowman

2. A _____ grows tall.

      sunlight   sunflower

3. The snow falls _____ .

      outside   inside

4. A _____ fell on my head.

      raindrop   rainbow

5. I put the letter in a _____ .

      mailbox   shoebox

Name _____

Names

You are a special person. Your name begins with a capital letter. We put a capital letter at the beginning of people's names because they are special.

Directions: Write your name. Did you remember to use a capital letter?

_____

- -

_____

Directions: Write each person's name. Use a capital letter at the beginning.

 Ted

- -

 Katie

- -

 Mike

- -

 Tim

- -

Write a friend's name. Use a capital letter at the beginning.

- -

Names: Days of the Week

The days of the week begin with capital letters.

Directions: Write the days of the week in the spaces below. Put them in order. Be sure to start with capital letters.

Tuesday	
Saturday	
Monday	
Friday	
Thursday	
Sunday	
Wednesday	

Name _____

Names: Months of the Year

The months of the year begin with capital letters.

Directions: Write the months of the year in order on the calendar below. Be sure to use capital letters.

January	December	April	May	October	June
September	February	July	March	November	August

_____	_____
_____	_____
_____	_____
_____	_____
_____	_____
_____	_____

More Than One

Directions: An **s** at the end of a word often means there is more than one. Look at each picture. Circle the correct word. Write the word on the line.

two

dog   dogs

_____

four

flower   flowers

_____

one

bikes   bike

_____

three

toys   toy

_____

a

lamb   lambs

_____

two

cat   cats

_____

Name _____

More Than One

Directions: Read the nouns under the pictures. Then write each noun under **One** or **More Than One**.

One

_____

_____

_____

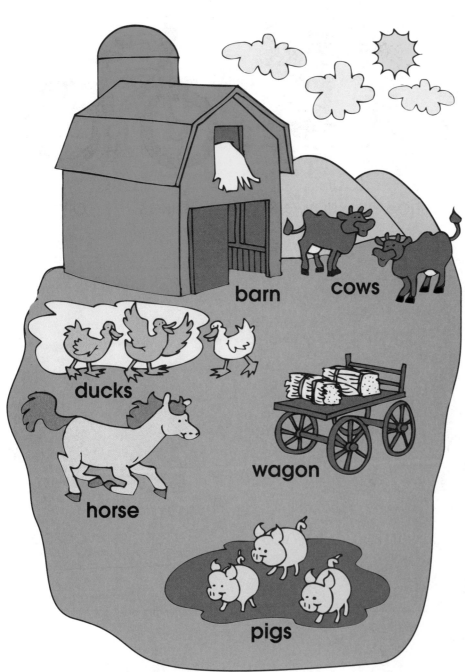

barn

cows

ducks

wagon

horse

pigs

More Than One

_____

_____

_____

READING COMPREHENSION

Name _____

More Than One

Directions: Choose the word which completes each sentence. Write each word on the line.

1. I have a _____ .

           dog   dogs

2. Four _____ are on the tree.

           apple   apples

3. I read two _____ today.

           book   books

4. My _____ is blue.

           bike   bikes

5. We saw lots of _____ at the zoo.

           monkey   monkeys

6. I have five _____ .

           balloon   balloons

Name _____

Riddles

Directions: Read the word. Trace and write it on the line. Then draw a line from the riddle to the animal it tells about.

long **long**

I am very big.
I lived a long, long time ago.
What am I?

giraffe

My neck is very long.
I eat leaves from trees.
What am I?

rabbit

I have long ears.
I hop very fast.
What am I?

dinosaur

Name _____

Riddles

Directions: Read the word and write it on the line. Then read each riddle and draw a line to the picture and word that tells about it.

house

_____

- - - - - - - - - - - - - - - - - - - -

I like to play.
I am little. I am soft.
What am I?

house

kitten

_____

- - - - - - - - - - - - - - - - - - - -

I am big.
You live in me.
What am I?

kitten

flower

_____

- - - - - - - - - - - - - - - - - - - -

I am pretty.
I am green and yellow.
What am I?

flower

pony

_____

- - - - - - - - - - - - - - - - - - - -

I can jump. I can run.
I am brown.
What am I?

pony

Name _____

Riddles

Directions: Write a word from the box to answer each riddle.

ice cream	book	chair	sun

There are many words in me.
I am fun to read.
What am I?

_____

I am soft and yellow.
You can sit on me.
What am I?

_____

I am in the sky in the day.
I am hot. I am yellow.
What am I?

_____

I am cold. I am sweet.
You like to eat me.
What am I?

_____

Name _____

Picture Clues

Directions: Read the sentence. Circle the word that makes sense. Use the picture clues to help you. Then write the word.

- .

I ride on a
bike   hike

- .

I ride on a
train   tree

- .

I ride in a
car   can

- .

I ride on a
bus   bug

- .

I ride in a
jar   jet

- .

I ride in a
took   truck

Name _____

Picture Clues

Directions: Read the sentence. Circle the word that makes sense. Use the picture clues to help you. Then write the word.

I see the _____ .

bird   book

I see the _____ .

fish   fork

I see the _____ .

dogs   dig

I see the _____ .

cats   coat

I see the _____ .

snake   snow

I see the _____ .

rat   rake

Comprehension

Directions: Look at the picture. Write the words from the box to finish the sentences.

frog	log	bird	fish	ducks

_____

The _____ can jump.

The turtle is on a _____ .

A _____ is in the tree.

The boy wants a _____ .

I see three _____ .

Comprehension

Directions: Read the poem. Write the correct words in the blanks.

A Poem

The hat was on a mat.
A cat sat on the hat.
Now the hat is flat.

The hat was on _____.

Who sat on the hat? _____

Now the hat is _____.

Name _____

Following Directions: Colour the Path

Directions: Colour the path the girl should take to go home. Use the sentences to help you.

1. Go to the school and turn left.

2. At the end of the street, turn right.

3. Walk past the park and turn right.

4. After you pass the pool, turn right.

Following Directions

Directions: Look at the pictures. Follow the directions in each box.

Draw a circle around the caterpillar.
Draw a line under the stick.

Draw an **X** on the mother bird.
Draw a triangle around the baby birds.

Draw a box around the rabbit.

Colour the flowers. Count the bees.
There are _____ bees.

Classifying

Directions: Classifying is sorting things into groups. Draw a circle around the pictures that answer the question.

What Can Swim?

What Can Fly?

Classifying: These Keep Me Warm

Directions: Colour the things that keep you warm.

socks

apple

lunch box

earmuffs

cookie

coat

hat

umbrella

gloves

book

Name _____

Classifying: Objects

Help Dan clean up the park.

Directions: Circle the litter. Underline the coins. Draw a box around the balls.

Name _____

Classifying: Things to Drink

Directions: Circle the pictures of things you can drink. Write the names of those things in the blanks.

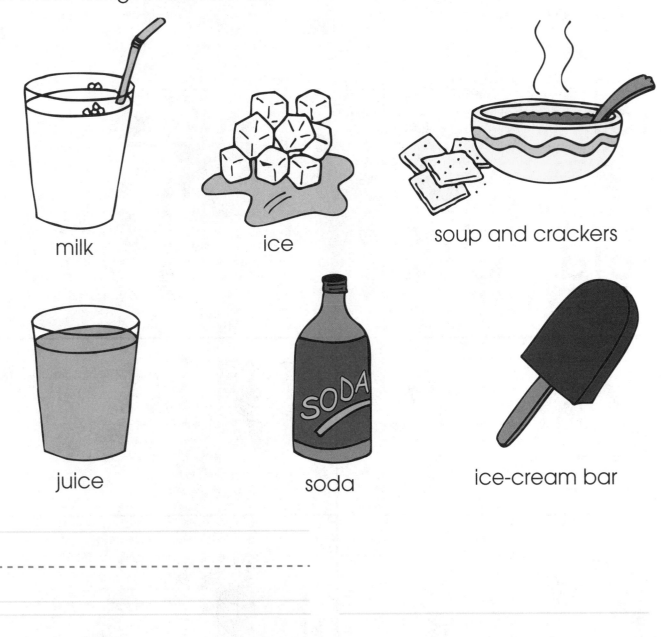

milk

ice

soup and crackers

juice

soda

ice-cream bar

Vocabulary

Directions: Read the words. Trace and write them on the lines. Look at each picture. Write **hot** or **cold** on the lines to show if it is hot or cold.

hot   hot --------------------------------

cold   cold --------------------------------

 - - - - - - - - - - - - - - - - - - -

 - - - - - - - - - - - - - - - - - - -

 - - - - - - - - - - - - - - - - - - -

 - - - - - - - - - - - - - - - - - - -

Vocabulary

Directions: Read the words. Trace and write them on the lines. Look at each picture and write **day** or **night** on the lines to show if they happen during the day or night.

day

night

Name _____

Classifying: Night and Day

Directions: Write the words from the box under the pictures they describe.

| stars | sun | moon | rays | dark | light | night | day |

- -

- -

- -

- -

Name _____

Classifying: Clowns and Balloons

Some words describe clowns. Some words describe balloons.

Directions: Read the words. Write the words that match in the correct columns.

float	laughs	hat	string
air	feet	pop	nose

clown

balloons

Name _____

Similarities: Objects

Directions: Circle the picture in each row that is most like the first picture.

Example:

potato

rose

tomato

tree

---

shirt

mittens

boots

jacket

---

whale

cat

dolphin

monkey

---

tiger

giraffe

lion

zebra

Similarities: Objects

Directions: Circle the picture in each row that is most like the first picture.

Example:

| carrot | jacks | bread | pea |

| baseball | sneakers | basketball | bat |

| store | school | home | bakery |

| kitten | dog | fox | cat |

Classifying: Food Groups

Directions: Colour the meats and eggs brown. Colour the fruits and vegetables green. Colour the breads tan. Colour the dairy foods (milk and cheese) yellow.

fish	bread	apple	cheese
crackers	carrot	orange	eggs
steaks	pear	milk	yogourt
ice cream	chicken	potato	pretzel

Name _____

Same and Different: These Don't Belong

Directions: Circle the pictures in each row that go together.

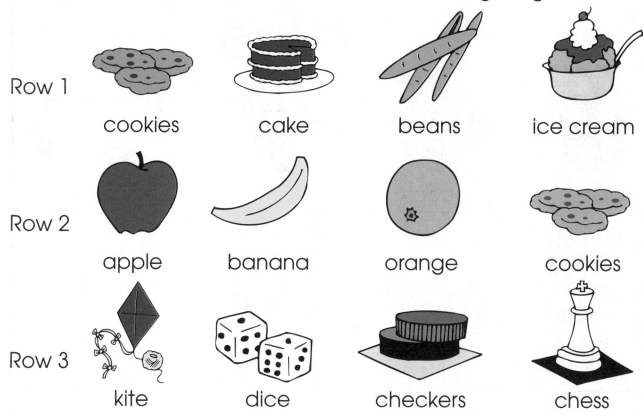

Row 1   cookies   cake   beans   ice cream

Row 2   apple   banana   orange   cookies

Row 3   kite   dice   checkers   chess

Directions: Write the names of the things that do not belong.

Row 1 _____

Row 2 _____

Row 3 _____

Name _____

Classifying: What Does Not Belong?

Directions: Draw an **X** on the picture that does not belong in each group.

fruit

| apple | peach | corn | watermelon |

wild animals

| bear | kitten | gorilla | lion |

pets

| cat | fish | elephant | dog |

flowers

| grass | rose | daisy | tulip |

Classifying: What Does Not Belong?

Directions: Draw an **X** on the word in each row that does not belong.

1.	flashlight	candle	radio	fire
2.	shirt	pants	coat	bat
3.	cow	car	bus	train
4.	beans	hot dog	ball	bread
5.	gloves	hat	book	boots
6.	fork	butter	cup	plate
7.	book	ball	bat	milk
8.	dogs	bees	flies	ants

Classifying: Objects

Directions: Write each word in the correct row at the bottom of the page.

airplane   drum   radio   plate   car   pencil

spoon   crayon   chalk   fork

television   boat

Things we ride in:

_____

- -

_____

Things we eat with:

_____

- -

_____

Things we draw with:

_____

- -

_____

Things we listen to:

_____

- -

_____

Name _____

Classifying: Names, Numbers, Animals, Colours

Directions: Write the words from the box next to the words they describe.

Joe	cat	blue	Tim
two	dog	red	ten
Sue	green	pig	six

Name Words _____

Number Words _____

Animal Words _____

Colour Words _____

Name _____

Classifying: Things That Belong Together

Directions: Circle the pictures in each row that belong together.

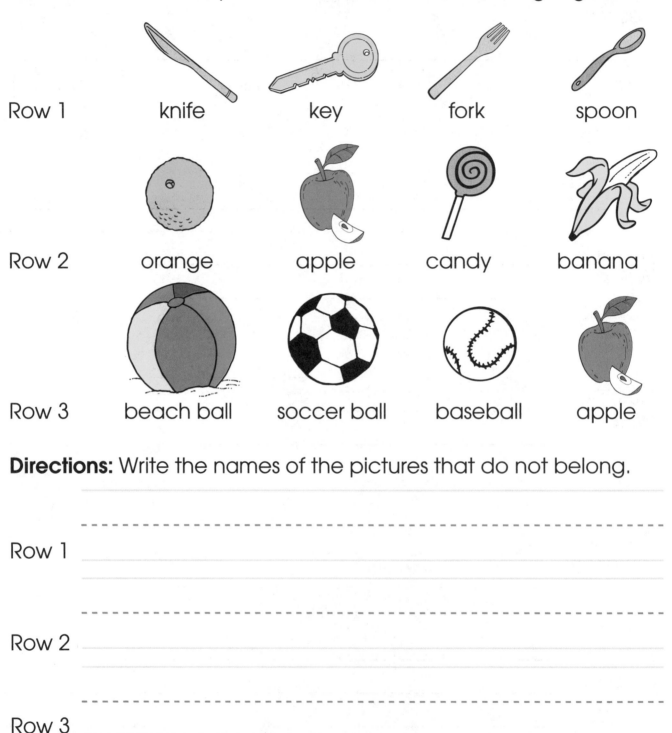

Row 1   knife   key   fork   spoon

Row 2   orange   apple   candy   banana

Row 3   beach ball   soccer ball   baseball   apple

Directions: Write the names of the pictures that do not belong.

Row 1 _____

Row 2 _____

Row 3 _____

Classifying: Why They Are Different

Directions: Look at your answers on page 90. Write why each object does not belong.

Row 1 _____

_____

Row 2 _____

_____

Row 3 _____

Directions: For each object, draw a group of pictures that belong with it.

candy bar

_____

lettuce

Name _____

Classifying: What Does Not Belong?

Directions: Circle the two things that do not belong in the picture. Write why they do not belong.

1. _____

_____

_____

2. _____

_____

Name _____

Sequencing: Fill the Glasses

Directions: Follow the instructions to fill each glass. Use crayons to draw your favourite drink in the ones that are full and half-full.

full

half-full

empty

empty

half-full

full

Sequencing: Raking Leaves

Directions: Write a number in each box to show the order of the story.

Sequencing: Make a Snowman!

Directions: Write the number of the sentence that goes with each picture in the box.

1. Roll a large snowball for the snowman's bottom.

2. Make another snowball and put it on top of the first.

3. Put the last snowball on top.

4. Dress the snowman.

Sequencing: A Recipe

Directions: Look at the recipe below. Put each step in order. Write **1, 2, 3** or **4** in the box.

HOW TO MAKE BREAD BUDDIES

Roll dough into balls and shapes. Connect pieces with a drop of water.

Mix 250 ml of water, 250 ml of salt and 750 ml of flour

Knead the dough.

Have an adult bake your bread buddy for 2-3 hours at 149°. Let it cool. Then paint it!

What kind of bread buddy did you make?

_____

Sequencing: How Flowers Grow

Directions: Read the story. Then write the steps to grow a flower.

First find a sunny spot. Then plant the seed. Water it. The flower will start to grow. Pull the weeds around it. Remember to keep giving the flower water. Enjoy your flower.

1. _____ .

2. _____ .

3. _____ .

4. _____ .

5. _____ .

Name _____

Comprehension: Apples

Directions: Read about apples. Then write the answers.

I like . Do you?   Some are red.

Some are green.   Some are yellow.

1. How many kinds of apples does the story tell about?

----

2. Name the kinds of apples.

----

3. What kind of apple do you like best?

Comprehension: Crayons

Directions: Read about crayons. Then write your answers.

Crayons come in many colours.
Some crayons are dark colours.
Some crayons are light colours.
All crayons have wax in them.

1. How many colours of crayons are there?   many

                                            few

2. Crayons come in _____ colours

   and _____ colours.

3. What do all crayons have in them?

   _____

   _____

Comprehension

Directions: Read the story. Write the words from the story that complete each sentence.

Jane and Bill like to play in the rain. They take off their shoes and socks.
They splash in the puddles.
It feels cold!
It is fun to splash!

Jane and Bill like to _____

_____

They take off their _____

They splash in _____

Do you like to splash in puddles?   Yes   No

Comprehension

Directions: Read the story. Write the words from the story that complete each sentence.

Ben and Sue have a bug.
It is red with black spots.
They call it Spot.
Spot likes to eat green
leaves and grass.
The children keep Spot in a box.

Ben and Sue have a _____ .

It is _____ with black spots.

The bug's name is _____ .

The bug eats _____ .

Name _____

Comprehension: Growing Flowers

Directions: Read about flowers. Then write the answers.

Some flowers grow in pots. Many flowers grow in flower beds. Others grow beside the road. Flowers begin from seeds. They grow into small buds. Then they open wide and bloom. Flowers are pretty!

1. Name two places flowers grow.

_____

_____

_____

2. Flowers begin from _____.

3. Then flowers grow into small _____.

4. Flowers then open wide and _____.

Name _____

Comprehension: Raking Leaves

Directions: Read about raking leaves. Then answer the questions.

I like to rake leaves. Do you? Leaves die each year. They get brown and dry. They fall from the trees. Then we rake them up.

1. What colour are leaves when they die?

----

2. What happens when they die?

----

3. What do we do when leaves fall?

Comprehension: Clocks

Directions: Read about clocks. Then answer the questions.

Ticking Clocks

Many clocks make two sounds. The sounds are tick and tock. Big clocks often make loud tick-tocks. Little clocks often make quiet tick-tocks. Sometimes people put little clocks in a box with a new puppy. The puppy likes the sound. The tick-tock makes the puppy feel safe.

1. What two sounds do many clocks make?

_____   _____

and _____

2. What kind of tick-tocks do big clocks make?

_____

_____

3. What kind of clock makes a new puppy feel safe?

_____

_____

Name _____

Comprehension: Soup

Directions: Read about soup. Then write the answers.

I Like Soup

Soup is good! It is good for you, too. We eat most kinds of soup hot. Some people eat cold soup in the summer. Carrots and beans are in some soups. Do you like crackers with soup?

1. Name two ways people eat soup.

_____   _____

_____   _____

2. Name two things that are in some soups.

_____   _____

_____   _____

3. Name the kind of soup you like best.

_____

_____

Name _____

Comprehension: The Teddy Bear Song

Do you know the Teddy Bear Song? It is very old!

Directions: Read the Teddy Bear Song. Then answer the questions.

Teddy bear, teddy bear, turn around.

Teddy bear, teddy bear, touch the ground.

Teddy bear, teddy bear, climb upstairs.

Teddy bear, teddy bear, say your prayers.

Teddy bear, teddy bear, turn out the light.

Teddy bear, teddy bear, say, "Good night!"

1. What is the first thing the teddy bear does?

_____

_____

2. What is the last thing the teddy bear does?

_____

_____

3. What would you name a teddy bear?

_____

_____

Name _____

Sequencing: Put Teddy Bear to Bed

Directions: Read the song about the teddy bear again. Write a number in each box to show the order of the story.

Name _____

Comprehension: A New Teddy Bear Song

Directions: Write words to make a new teddy bear song. Act out your new song with your teddy bear as you read it.

_____

_____

Teddy bear, teddy bear, turn _____ .

_____

Teddy bear, teddy bear, touch the _____ .

_____

Teddy bear, teddy bear, climb _____ .

_____

Teddy bear, teddy bear, turn out _____ .

_____

Teddy bear, teddy bear, say, _____ .

Sequencing: Petting a Cat

Directions: Read the story. Then write the answers.

Do you like cats? I do. To pet a cat, move slowly. Hold out your hand. The cat will come to you. Then pet its head. Do not grab a cat! It will run away.

To pet a cat . . .

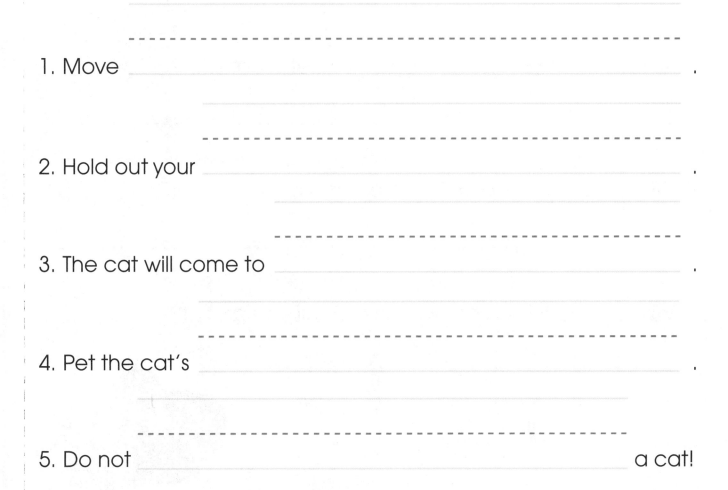

1. Move _____.

2. Hold out your _____.

3. The cat will come to _____.

4. Pet the cat's _____.

5. Do not _____ a cat!

Name _____

Comprehension: Cats

Directions: Read the story about cats again. Then write the answers.

1. What is a good title for the story?

_____

_____

2. The story tells you how to _____

3. What part of your body should you pet a cat with?

_____

_____

4. Why should you move slowly to pet a cat?

_____

_____

5. Why do you think a cat will run away if you grab it?

_____

_____

_____

Name _____

Comprehension: Cats

Directions: Look at the pictures and read about four cats. Then write the correct name beside each cat.

Fluffy, Blackie and Tiger are playing. Tom is sleeping. Blackie has spots. Tiger has stripes.

Name _____

Same and Different: Cats

Directions: Compare the picture of the cats on page 111 to this picture. Write a word from the box to tell what is different about each cat.

purple ball	green bow	blue brush	red collar

1. Tom is wearing a _____ .

2. Blackie has a _____ .

3. Fluffy is wearing a _____ .

4. Tiger has a _____ .

Name _____

Comprehension: Tigers

Directions: Read about tigers. Then write the answers.

Tigers sleep during the day. They hunt at night. Tigers eat meat. They hunt deer. They like to eat wild pigs. If they cannot find meat, tigers will eat fish.

1. When do tigers sleep?

_____

_____

2. Name two things tigers eat.

_____

_____

_____

3. When do tigers hunt?

Following Directions: Tiger Puzzle

Directions: Read the story about tigers again. Then complete the puzzle.

Across:

1. When tigers cannot get meat, they eat _____ .

3. The food tigers like best is _____ .

4. Tigers like to eat this meat: wild _____ .

Down:

2. Tigers do this during the day.

Name _____

Following Directions: Draw a Tiger

Directions: Follow directions to complete the picture of the tiger.

1. Draw black stripes on the tiger's body and tail.

2. Colour the tiger's tongue red.

3. Draw claws on the feet.

4. Draw a black nose and two black eyes on the tiger's face.

5. Colour the rest of the tiger orange.

6. Draw tall, green grass for the tiger to sleep in.

Comprehension: Write a Party Invitation

Directions: Read about the party. Then complete the invitation.

The party will be at Dog's house. The party will start at 1:00 P.M. It will last 2 hours. Write your birthday for the date of the party.

Party Invitation

Where: -

Date: -

Time It Begins: -

Time It Ends: -

- -

Directions: On the last line, write something else about the party.

Sequencing: Pig Gets Ready

Directions: Number the pictures of Pig getting ready for the party to show the order of the story.

What kind of party do you think Pig is going to? _____

Name _____

Comprehension: An Animal Party

Directions: Use the picture for clues. Write words from the box to answer the questions.

bear	cat
dog	elephant
giraffe	hippo
pig	tiger

1. Which animals have bow ties?

_____

_____

2. Which animal has a hat?

_____

_____

3. Which animal has a striped shirt?

Classifying: Party Items

Directions: Draw a ☐ around objects that are food for the party. Draw a △ around the party guests. Draw a ◯ around the objects used for fun at the party.

ice cream

candy

games

tiger

noise makers

cake

garbage can

cat

hat

glasses

candle

bear

juice

balloons

giraffe

pig

potato chips

hippo

Comprehension: Rhymes

Directions: Read about words that rhyme. Then circle the answers.

Words that rhyme have the same end sounds. "Wing" and "sing" rhyme. "Boy" and "toy" rhyme. "Dime" and "time" rhyme. Can you think of other words that rhyme?

1. Words that rhyme have the same   end sounds.

                                                                        end letters.

TREE, SEE
SHOE, BLUE
KITE, BITE
MAKE, TAKE
FLY, BUY

2. Time rhymes with   "tree."

                                          "dime."

Directions: Write one rhyme for each word.

wing

_____

boy

_____

dime

_____

pink

_____

Rhyming Words

Many poems have rhyming words. The rhyming words are usually at the end of the line.

Directions: Complete the poem with words from the box.

My Glue

I spilled my _____ .

I felt _____ .

What could I _____ ?

Hey! I have a _____ !

I'll make it _____ .

The cleanest you've _____ .

No one will _____ .

Wouldn't that be _____ ?

blue	clue	scream	seen
glue	do	clean	mean

Name _____

Classifying: Rhymes

Directions: Circle the pictures in each row that rhyme.

Row 1

Row 2

Row 3

Directions: Write the names of the pictures that do not rhyme.

These words do not rhyme:

Row 1	Row 2	Row 3
- - - - - - - - -	- - - - - - - - -	- - - - - - - - -

Predicting: Words and Pictures

Directions: Complete each story by choosing the correct picture. Draw a line from the story to the picture.

1. Shawnda got her books. She went

   to the bus stop. Shawnda got

   on the bus.

2. Marco planted a seed. He watered it.

   He pulled the weeds around it.

3. Abraham's dog was barking.

   Abraham got out the dog food.

   He put it in the dog bowl.

Name _____

Predicting: Story Ending

Directions: Read the story. Draw a picture in the last box to complete the story.

That's my ball.   I got it first.

It's mine!

Name _____

Predicting: Story Ending

Directions: Read the story. Draw a picture in the last box to complete the story.

Marco likes to paint.   He likes to help his dad.

He is tired when he's finished.

Name _____

Predicting: Story Ending

Directions: Read each story. Circle the sentence that tells how the story will end.

Ann was riding her bike. She saw a dog in the park. She stopped to pet it. Ann left to go home.

The dog went swimming.

The dog followed Ann.

The dog went home with a cat.

Antonio went to a baseball game. A baseball player hit a ball toward him. He reached out his hands.

The player caught the ball.

The ball bounced on a car.

Antonio caught the ball.

Name _____

Making Inferences: Baseball

Traci likes baseball. She likes to win. Traci's team does not win.

Directions: Circle the correct answers.

1. Traci likes

 football.   soccer.   baseball.

2. Traci likes to

 win.   lose.

3. Traci uses a bat.

Yes   No

4. Traci is

 happy.   sad.

Making Inferences: The Stars

Lynn looks at the stars. She sings a song about them. She makes a wish on them. The stars help Lynn sleep.

Directions: Circle the correct answers.

1. Lynn likes the

moon.

sun.

stars.

2. What song do you think she sings?

Row, Row, Row Your Boat

Twinkle, Twinkle Little Star

Happy Birthday to You

3. What does Lynn "make" on the stars?

a wish   a spaceship   lunch

Name _____

Making Inferences: Feelings

Directions: Read each story. Choose a word from the box to show how each person feels.

happy	excited	sad	mad

1. Andy and Sam were best friends. Sam and his family moved far away. How does Sam feel?

_____

- - - - - - - - - - - - - -

_____

2. Deana could not sleep. It was the night before her birthday party. How does Deana feel?

_____

- - - - - - - - - - - - - -

_____

3. Jacob let his baby brother play with his teddy bear. His brother lost the bear. How does Jacob feel?

_____

- - - - - - - - - - - - - -

_____

4. Kia picked flowers for her mom. Her mom smiled when she got them. How does Kia feel?

_____

- - - - - - - - - - - - - -

_____

Name _____

Books

Directions: What do you know about books? Use the words in the box below to help fill in the lines.

title	book	author
illustrator	pages	left to right
fun	library	glossary

The name of the book is the _____ .

_____ is the direction we read.

The person who wrote the words is the _____

Reading is _____ !

There are many books in the _____ .

The person who draws the pictures is the _____

The _____ is a kind of dictionary in the book to help you find the meanings of words.

ENGLISH

TALL

TALLEST

TALLER

Name _____

Nouns

A noun is a word that names a person, place or thing. When you read a sentence, the noun is what the sentence is about.

Directions: Complete each sentence with a noun.

The _____ is fat.

My _____ is blue.

The _____ has apples.

The _____ is hot.

Nouns

Directions: Write these naming words in the correct box.

| store | zoo | child | baby | teacher | table |
| cat | park | gym | woman | sock | horse |

Person

_____ _____

_____ _____

Place

_____ _____

_____ _____

Thing

_____ _____

_____ _____

Things That Go Together

Some nouns name things that go together.

Directions: Draw a line to match the nouns on the left with the things they go with on the right.

toothpaste

pencil

salt

shoe

soap

pillow

washcloth

sock

toothbrush

pepper

paper

bed

Name _____

Things That Go Together

Directions: Draw a line to connect the objects that go together.

Verbs

Verbs are words that tell what a person or a thing can do.

Example: The girl pats the dog.

The word **pats** is the verb. It shows action.

Directions: Draw a line between the verbs and the pictures that show the action.

eat

run

sleep

swim

sing

hop

Name _____

Verbs

Directions:
Look at the picture and read the words. Write an action word in each sentence below.

swing

rings

kick

run

talk

1. The two boys like to _____ together.

2. The children _____ the soccer ball.

3. Some children like to _____ on the swing.

4. The girl can _____ very fast.

5. The teacher _____ the bell.

Words That Describe

Describing words tell us more about a person, place or thing.

Directions: Read the words in the box. Choose the word that describes the picture. Write it next to the picture.

happy	round	sick	cold	long

Name _____

Words That Describe

Directions: Read the words in the box. Choose the word that describes the picture. Write it next to the picture.

wet	round	funny	soft	sad	tall

_____

_____

_____

_____

_____

_____

Words That Describe

Directions: Circle the describing word in each sentence. Draw a line from the sentence to the picture.

1. The hungry dog is eating.

2. The tiny bird is flying.

3. Horses have long legs.

4. She is a fast runner.

5. The little boy was lost.

Words That Describe: Colours and Numbers

Colours and numbers can describe nouns.

Directions: Underline the describing word in each sentence. Draw a picture to go with each sentence.

A yellow moon was in the sky.

Two worms are on the road.

The tree had red apples.

The girl wore a blue dress.

Name _____

Sequencing: Comparative Adjectives

Directions: Look at each group of pictures. Write 1, 2 or 3 under the picture to show where it should be.

Example:

tallest __3__ **tall** __1__ **taller** __2__

small _____ **smallest** _____ **smaller** _____

biggest _____ **big** _____ **bigger** _____

wider _____ **wide** _____ **widest** _____

Sequencing: Comparative Adjectives

Directions: Look at the pictures in each row. Write 1, 2 or 3 under the picture to show where it should be.

shortest _____   **shorter** _____   **short** _____

longest _____   **longer** _____   **long** _____

happy _____   **happier** _____   **happiest** _____

hotter _____   **hot** _____   **hottest** _____

Synonyms

Synonyms are words that mean almost the same thing. **Start** and **begin** are synonyms.

Directions: Find the synonyms that describe each picture. Write the words in the boxes below the picture.

small   funny   large   sad   silly   little   big   unhappy

Similarities: Synonyms

Directions: Circle the word in each row that is most like the first word in the row.

Example:

grin		(smile)	frown	mad
bag		jar	sack	box
cat		fruit	animal	flower
apple		rot	cookie	fruit
around		circle	square	dot
brown		tan	black	red
bird		dog	cat	duck
bee		fish	ant	snake

Synonyms

Directions: Read each sentence and look at the underlined word. Circle the word that means the same thing. Write the new words.

1. The boy was <u>mad</u>.	happy	angry	pup
2. The <u>dog</u> is brown.	pup	cat	rat
3. I like to <u>scream</u>.	soar	mad	shout
4. The bird can <u>fly</u>.	soar	jog	warm
5. The girl can <u>run</u>.	sleep	jog	shout
6. I am <u>hot</u>.	warm	cold	soar

Name _____

Similarities: Synonyms

Directions: Read the story. Write a word on the line that means almost the same as the word under the line.

_____

_____

Dan went to the _____ .
                        store

_____

_____

He wanted to buy _____ .
                        food

_____

_____

He walked very _____ .
                    quickly

The store had what he wanted. _____

_____

He bought it using _____ .
                        dimes

_____

_____

Instead of walking home, Dan _____ .
                                    jogged

Antonyms

Antonyms are words that are opposites. **Hot** and **cold** are antonyms.
Directions: Draw a line between the antonyms.

closed

below

full

empty

above

old

new

open

Name _____

Opposites

Directions: Draw lines to connect the words that are opposites.

up	wet
over	down
dry	dirty
clean	under

Name _____

Opposites

Opposites are things that are different in every way.

Directions: Draw a line between the opposites.

day

happy

big

open

front

little

closed

night

back

sad

Name _____

Opposites

Directions: Circle the picture in each row that is the opposite of the first picture.

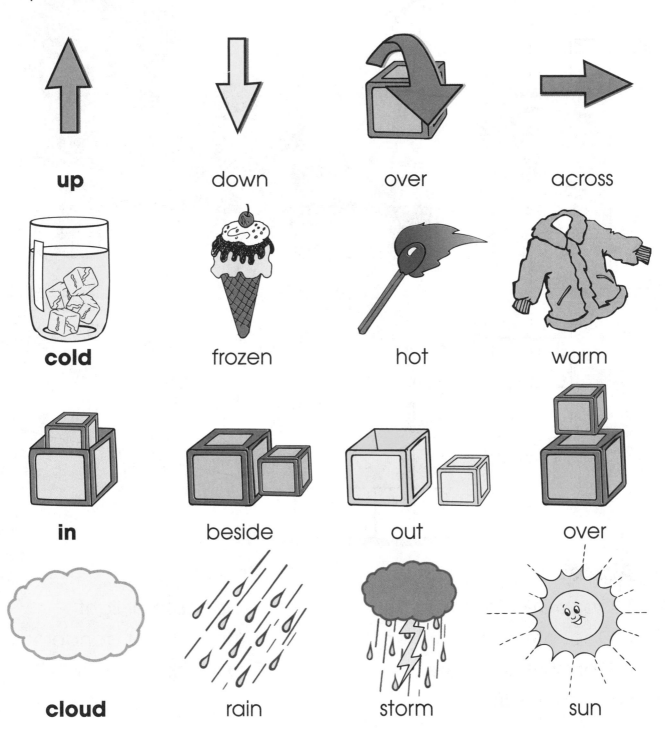

| up | down | over | across |

| cold | frozen | hot | warm |

| in | beside | out | over |

| cloud | rain | storm | sun |

151 Complete Early Skills Grade 1

GRADE 1

Name _____

Opposites

Directions: Read each clue. Write the answers in the puzzle.

high   yes   left
heavy   tight
safe   full

Across:

1. Opposite of low
2. Opposite of no
4. Opposite of empty
6. Opposite of loose

Down:

1. Opposite of light
3. Opposite of dangerous
5. Opposite of right

Homophones

Homophones are words that **sound** the same but are spelled differently and mean something different. **Blew** and **blue** are homophones.

Directions: Look at the word pairs. Choose the word that describes the picture. Write the word on the line next to the picture.

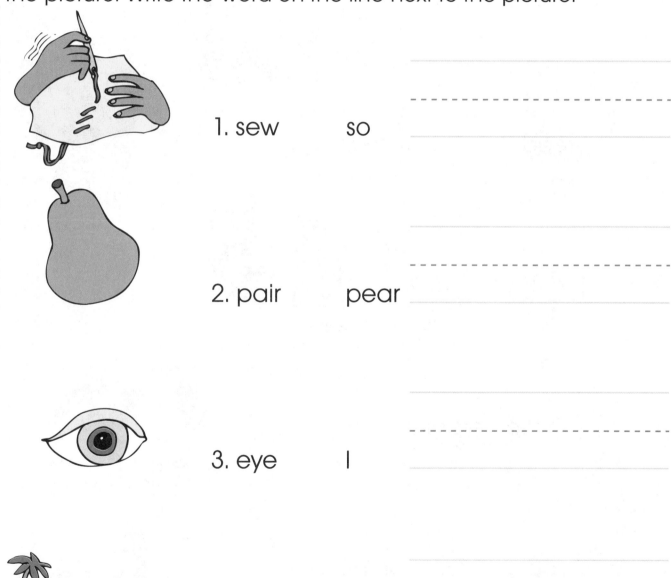

1. sew   so

2. pair   pear

3. eye   I

4. see   sea

Name _____

Homophones

Directions: Read each sentence. Underline the two words that sound the same but are spelled differently and mean something different.

1. Tom ate eight grapes.

2. Becky read *Little Red Riding Hood.*

3. I went to buy two dolls.

4. Five blue feathers blew in the wind.

5. Would you get wood for the fire?

Name _____

Sentences

Sentences begin with capital letters.

Directions: Read the sentences and write them below. Begin each sentence with a capital letter.

Example: the cat is fat.

The cat is fat.

my dog is big.

_____

the boy is sad.

_____

bikes are fun!

_____

dad can bake.

_____

Name _____

Word Order

If you change the order of the words in a sentence, you can change the meaning of the sentence.

Directions: Read the sentences. Draw a circle around the sentence that describes the picture.

Example:

(The fox jumped over the dogs.)
The dogs jumped over the fox.

1. The cat watched the bird.
    The bird watched the cat.

2. The girl looked at the boy.
    The boy looked at the girl.

3. The turtle ran past the rabbit.
    The rabbit ran past the turtle.

Word Order

Directions: Look at the picture. Put the words in order. Write the sentences on the lines below.

1. We made lemonade. some
2. good. It was
3. We the sold lemonade.
4. cost It five cents.
5. fun. We had

1. _____

2. _____

3. _____

4. _____

5. _____

Name _____

Telling Sentences

Directions: Read the sentences and write them below. Begin each sentence with a capital letter. End each sentence with a period.

1. most children like pets
2. some children like dogs
3. some children like cats
4. some children like snakes
5. some children like all animals

1. _____

2. _____

3. _____

4. _____

5. _____

Telling Sentences

Directions: Read the sentences and write them below.
Begin each sentence with a capital letter.
End each sentence with a period.

1. i like to go to the store with Mom
2. we go on Friday
3. i get to push the cart
4. i get to buy the cookies
5. i like to help Mom

1. _____

2. _____

3. _____

4. _____

5. _____

Asking Sentences

Directions: Write the first word of each asking sentence. Be sure to begin each question with a capital letter. End each question with a question mark.

1. _____ you like the zoo   **do**

2. _____ much does it cost   **how**

3. _____ you feed the ducks   **can**

4. _____ you see the monkeys   **will**

5. _____ time will you eat lunch   **what**

Name _____

Asking Sentences

Directions: Read the asking sentences. Write the sentences below. Begin each sentence with a capital letter. End each sentence with a question mark.

1. what game will we play
2. do you like to read
3. how old are you
4. who is your best friend
5. can you tie your shoes

1.

2.

3.

4.

5.

Periods and Question Marks

Directions: Put a period or a question mark at the end of each sentence below.

1. Do you like parades

2. The clowns lead the parade

3. Can you hear the band

4. The balloons are big

5. Can you see the horses

Name _____

Is and Are

We use **is** in sentences about one person or one thing. We use **are** in sentences about more than one person or thing.

Example: The dog **is** barking.
The dogs **are** barking.

Directions: Write **is** or **are** in the sentences below.

1. Jim _____ playing baseball.

2. Fred and Sam _____ good friends.

3. Cupcakes _____ my favourite treat.

4. Lisa _____ a good soccer player.

Name _____

Is and Are

Directions: Write **is** or **are** in the sentences below.
Example: Lisa __**is**__ sleeping.

1. Cats and dogs _____ good pets.

2. Bill _____ my best friend.

3. Apples _____ good to eat.

4. We _____ going to the zoo.

5. Pedro _____ coming to my house.

6. When _____ you all going to the zoo?

Name _____

Colour Names

Directions: Trace the letters to write the name of each colour. Then write the name again by yourself.

Example:

orange   orange

blue

green

yellow

red

brown

Colour Names: Sentences

Directions: Use the colour words to complete these sentences. Then put a period at the end.

Example: My new are **orange.**

green tree	blue bike	yellow chick	red ball

1. The baby is _____ ☐

2. This is _____ ☐

3. My is big and _____ ☐

4. My sister's is _____ ☐

Name _____

Animal Names

Directions: Fill in the missing letters for each word.

Example:

fr og   fr og

fi _ _   f _ sh

d _ g   _ og

b _ _ d   _ ir _

c _ t   _ a _

Animal Names: Sentences

A **sentence** tells about something.

Directions: These sentences tell about animals. Write the word that completes each sentence.

Example:

My **frog** jumps high.

1. I take my _____ for a walk.

2. My _____ lives in water.

3. My _____ can sing.

4. My _____ has a long tail.

Name _____

Things That Go

Directions: Trace the letters to write the name of each thing. Write each name again by yourself. Then colour the pictures.

Example:

 car   car

 truck

 train

 bike

 plane

Name _____

Things That Go: Sentences

Directions: These sentences tell about things that go. Write the word that completes each sentence.

Example:

The **car** is in the garage.

1. The _____ was at the farm.

2. My _____ had a flat tire.

3. The _____ flew high.

4. The _____ went fast.

Name _____

Clothing Words

Directions: Trace the letters to write the name of each clothing word. Then write each name again by yourself.

Example:

shirt   shirt

pants

jacket

socks

shoes

dress

hat

Name _____

Clothing Words: Sentences

Directions: Some of these sentences tell a whole idea. Others have something missing. If something is missing, draw a line to the word that completes the sentence. Put a period at the end of each sentence.

Example:

She is wearing a polka-dot

holes

1. The baseball player wore a

2. His pants were torn.

dress .

3. The socks had

4. The jacket had blue buttons.

hat

5. The shoes were brown.

Name _____

Food Names

Directions: Trace the letters to write the name of each food word. Write each name again by yourself. Then colour the pictures.

Example: bread **bread**

 cookie

 apple

 cake

 milk

 egg

Name _____

Food Names: Asking Sentences

An **asking sentence** asks a question. Asking sentences end with a question mark.

Directions: Write each sentence on the line. Begin each sentence with a capital letter. Put a period at the end of the telling sentences and a question mark at the end of the asking sentences.

Example: do you like cake

Do you like cake?

1. the cow has spots

_____

_____

2. is that cookie good

_____

_____

3. she ate the apple

_____

_____

Name _____

Number Words

Directions: Trace the letters to write the name of each number. Write the numbers again by yourself. Then colour the number pictures.

Example:

1 one   **one**

2 two

3 three

4 four

5 five

6 six

7 seven

8 eight

9 nine

10 ten

Number Words: Asking Sentences

Directions: Use a number word to answer each question.

one	five	seven	three	eight

1. How many trees are there?

2. How many flowers are there?

3. How many presents are there?

4. How many clocks are there?

5. How many forks are there?

Name _____

Action Words

Action words tell things we can do.

Directions: Trace the letters to write each action word. Then write the action word again by yourself.

Example:

 sleep   **sleep**

 run

 make

 ride

 play

 stop

Action Words: More Than One

To show more than one of something, add **s** to the end of the word.

Example: one cat   two cats

Directions: In each sentence, add **s** to show more than one. Then write the action word that completes each sentence.

| sit | jump | stop | ride |

Example:

 The frog **s sleep** in the sun.

1. The boy _____ _____ on the fence.

2. The car _____ _____ at the sign.

3. The girl _____ _____ in the water.

4. The dog _____ _____ in the wagon.

Name _____

Action Words: Asking Sentences

Directions: Write an asking sentence about each picture. Begin each sentence with **can**. Add an action word. Begin each asking sentence with a capital letter and end it with a question mark.

Example:

I with you can

Can I sit with you?

she can

_____

- -

with you can I

_____

- -

can she fast

_____

- -

Sense Words

Directions: Circle the word that is spelled correctly. Then write the correct spelling in the blank.

Example:

tast
(taste)
tste

touch
tuch
touh

smel
smll
smell

her
hear
har

see
se
sea

Sense Words: Sentences

Directions: Read each sentence and write the correct words in the blanks.

Example:

taste
mouth   I can **taste** things with my **mouth**.

touch
hands   1. I can _____ things with my _____.

nose
smell   2. I can _____ things with my _____.

hear
ears   3. I can _____ with my _____.

see
eyes   4. I can _____ things with my _____.

GRADE 1

Name _____

Weather Words: Beginning Sounds

Directions: Say the sound of the letter at the beginning of each row. Find the pictures in each row that begin with the same letter. Write the letter under the pictures.

Example:

s   _____   S   S   _____

w   _____   _____   _____   _____

c   _____   _____   _____   _____

p   _____   _____   _____   _____

s   _____   _____   _____   _____

r   _____   _____   _____   _____

Name _____

Weather Words: Sentences

Directions: Write the weather word that completes each sentence. Put a period at the end of the telling sentences and a question mark at the end of the asking sentences.

Example:

Do flowers grow in the _____ sun ?

rain	water	wet	hot

1. The sun makes me _____ ☐

2. When it rains, the grass gets _____ ☐

3. Do you think it will _____ on our picnic ☐

4. Should you drink the _____ from the rain ☐

Name _____

My World

Directions: Fill in the missing letters for each word.

tr_ee_   tree

gr_ss   __ __ a __ __

fl__ __ __ er   __ __ __ ow __ __

p_ nd   __ __ o __

s_ nd   __ __ a __ __

sk__   __ __ y

185

Name _____

My World

Directions: The letters in the words below are mixed up. Unscramble the letters and write each word correctly.

etre _____

srags _____

loefwr _____

dnop _____

dnsa _____

yks _____

Name _____

My World: Sentences

Directions: Write the word that completes each sentence. Put a period at the end of the telling sentences and a question mark at the end of the asking sentences.

Example: Does the sun shine on the ___flowers___?

tree	grass	pond	sand	sky

1. The _____ was full of dark clouds ☐

2. Can you climb the _____ ☐

3. Did you see the duck in the _____ ☐

4. Is the child playing in the _____ ☐

5. The _____ in the yard was tall ☐

Name _____

The Parts of My Body: Sentences

Directions: Write the word that completes each sentence. Put a period at the end of the telling sentences and a question mark at the end of the asking sentences.

Example: I wear my hat on my **head.**

arms	legs	feet	hands

1. How strong are your _____ ☐

2. You wear shoes on your _____ ☐

3. If you're happy and you know it, clap your _____ ☐

4. My pants covered my _____ ☐

Name _____

The Parts of My Body: Sentences

Directions: Read the sentence parts below. Draw a line from the first part of the sentence to the second part that completes it.

1. I give big hugs

with my arms.

with my car.

2. My feet

drive the car.

got wet in the rain.

3. I have a bump

on my head.

on my coat.

4. My mittens

keep my arms warm.

keep my hands warm.

5. I can jump high

using my legs.

using a spoon.

Name _____

The Parts of My Body: Sentences

Directions: Read the two sentences on each line and draw a line between them. Then write each sentence again on the lines below. Begin each sentence with a capital letter, and end each one with a period or a question mark.

Example: wash your hands│they are dirty

Wash your hands.
They are dirty.

1. you have big arms are you very strong

- -

_____

- -

2. I have two feet I can run fast

- -

_____

- -

MATH

Number Recognition

Directions: Write the numbers 1-10. Colour the bear.

Name _____

Number Recognition

Directions: Count the number of objects in each group. Draw a line to the correct number.

1

2

3

4

5

6

7

8

9

10

Name _____

Counting

Directions: How many are there of each shape? Write the answers in the boxes. The first one is done for you.

Counting

Directions: How many are there of each picture? Write the answers in the boxes. The first one is done for you.

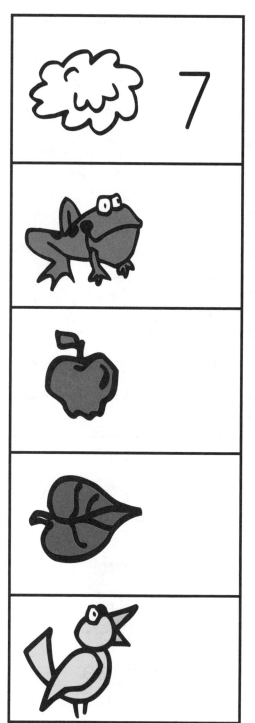

Name _____

Number Word Find

Directions: Find the number words 0 through 12 hidden in the box.

```
t  e  a  z  w  z  x  a  b  i  g  t  e  n
o  l  z  r  b  e  r  e  v  e  d  l  a  j
t  w  e  l  v  e  a  b  o  n  e  c  d  z
i  a  r  p  q  d  p  s  u  j  x  e  i  w
c  f  o  p  l  s  c  k  i  q  u  i  i  o
m  s  t  f  v  i  o  e  t  t  f  g  h  d
t  n  u  w  u  x  g  z  w  h  g  h  r  o
n  i  n  e  k  f  d  f  o  u  r  t  j  f
a  s  g  l  q  c  w  k  o  s  n  v  m  i
n  y  c  e  b  o  n  h  h  p  o  m  p  v
b  e  x  v  s  s  e  v  e  n  w  e  n  e
t  h  r  e  e  r  t  a  l  j  k  x  q  z
m  o  a  n  e  n  i  m  u  t  w  a  y  x
```

Words to find:

zero	four	eight	eleven
one	five	nine	twelve
two	six	ten	
three	seven		

Name _____

Number Words

Directions: Number the buildings from one to six.

Directions: Draw a line from the word to the number.

two	1
five	3
six	5
four	6
one	2
three	4

Name _____

Number Words

Directions: Number the buildings from five to ten.

Directions: Draw a line from the word to the number.

nine   8

seven   10

five   7

eight   5

six   9

ten   6

Number Recognition Review

Directions: Match the correct number of objects with the number.
Then match the number with the word.

	1	four
	2	ten
	3	two
	4	six
	5	one
	6	nine
	7	three
	8	eight
	9	five
	10	seven

Name _____

Sequencing Numbers

Sequencing is putting numbers in the correct order.

1, 2, 3, 4, 5, 6, 7, 8, 9, 10

Directions: Write the missing numbers.

Example: 4, ___5___ , 6

3, _____ , 5   7, _____ , 9   8, _____ , 10

6, _____ , 8   _____ , 3, 4   _____ , 5, 6

5, 6, _____   _____ , 6, 7   _____ , 3, 4

_____ , 4, 5   _____ , 7, 8   5, _____ , 7

2, 3, _____   1, 2, _____   7, 8, _____

2, _____ , 4   _____ , 2, 3   4, _____ , 6

6, 7, _____   3, 4, _____   1, _____ , 3

7, 8, _____   _____ , 3, 4   _____ , 9, 10

Name _____

Number Match

Directions: Cut out the pictures and number words below. Mix them up and match them again.

one	(flower)	two	eight
(wagons)	(worms)	five	(bees)
(dogs)	three	(clocks)	nine
four	(drums)	seven	(frogs)
(globes)	six	(birds)	ten

Page is blank for cutting exercise on previous page.

Name _____

Number Crossword Puzzle

Directions: Write the correct number word in the boxes provided.

Across
2. 4
3. 8
5. 2
7. 7
9. 10

Down
1. 0
2. 5
4. 3
6. 1
7. 6
8. 9

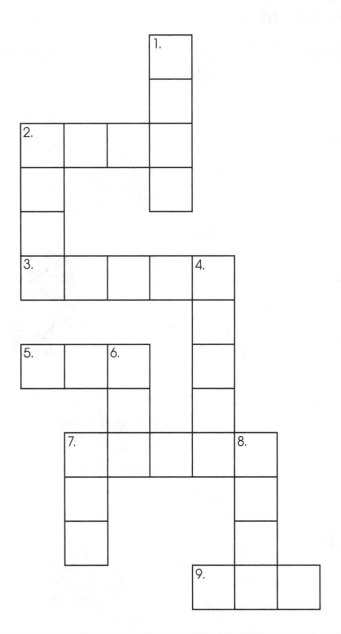

one	two	three	four	five
●	●●	●●●	●●●●	●●●●●

six	seven	eight	nine	ten	zero
●●● ●●●	●●●● ●●●	●●●● ●●●●	●●●●● ●●●●	●●●●● ●●●●●	

Ordinal Numbers

Ordinal numbers are used to indicate order in a series, such as **first**, **second** or **third**.

Directions: Draw a line to the picture that corresponds to the ordinal number in the left column.

eighth

third

sixth

ninth

seventh

second

fourth

first

fifth

tenth

1st

7th

10th

2nd

4th

6th

8th

9th

3rd

5th

Name _____

Ordinal Numbers

Directions: Draw an **X** on the first vegetable, draw a circle around the second vegetable, and draw a square around the third vegetable.

Directions: Write the ordinal number below the picture.

✂ **Cut** the children apart. Mix them up. Then put them back in the correct order.

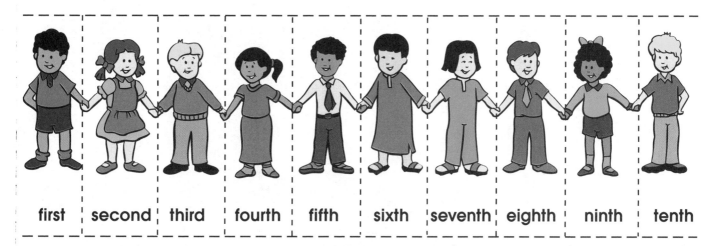

| first | second | third | fourth | fifth | sixth | seventh | eighth | ninth | tenth |

Page is blank for cutting exercise on previous page.

Name _____

Sequencing: At the Movies

Directions: The children are watching a movie. Read the sentences. Cut out the pictures below. Glue them where they belong in the picture.

1. The first child is eating popcorn.
2. The third child is eating candy.
3. The fourth child has a cup of fruit punch.
4. The second child is eating a big pretzel.

Page is blank for cutting exercise on previous page.

Sequencing: Standing in Line

Directions: These children are waiting to see a movie. Look at them and follow the instructions.

1. Colour the person who is first in line yellow.

2. Colour the person who is last in line brown.

3. Colour the person who is second in line pink.

4. Circle the person who is at the end of the line.

Name _____

Addition 1, 2

Addition means "putting together" or adding two or more numbers to find the sum. "+" is a plus sign. It means to add the 2 numbers. "=" is an equals sign. It tells how much they are together.

Directions: Count the cats and tell how many.

 + = _____

 + = _____

 + = _____

Name _____

Addition

Directions: Count the shapes and write the numbers below to tell how many in all.

 + =

- - - - - - -   - - - - - - -   - - - - - - -

◯◯ + ◯ =

- - - - - - -   - - - - - - -   - - - - - - -

▢ + ▢▢ = ▢▢▢

- - - - - - -   - - - - - - -   - - - - - - -

☆☆☆ + ☆ =

- - - - - - -   - - - - - - -   - - - - - - -

Name _____

Addition

Directions: Draw the correct number of dots next to the numbers in each problem. Add up the number of dots to find your answer.

Example:

$$\begin{array}{r} 3 \\ +2 \\ \hline 5 \end{array}$$

$2 + 2 = \underline{4}$

$\begin{array}{r} 4 \\ +2 \\ \hline \end{array}$	$1 + 5 = \underline{}$
$\begin{array}{r} 3 \\ +1 \\ \hline \end{array}$	$4 + 3 = \underline{}$
$\begin{array}{r} 6 \\ +2 \\ \hline \end{array}$	$5 + 3 = \underline{}$

Addition 3, 4, 5, 6

Directions: Practise writing the numbers and then add. Draw dots to help, if needed.

3

4

5

- - - - - - - - - - - - - - - -

6

- - - - - - - - - - - - - - - -

$$\begin{array}{r} 2 \\ +4 \\ \hline \end{array} \qquad \begin{array}{r} 1 \\ +4 \\ \hline \end{array}$$

$$\begin{array}{r} 3 \\ +2 \\ \hline \end{array} \qquad \begin{array}{r} 1 \\ +2 \\ \hline \end{array}$$

Addition 4, 5, 6, 7

Directions: Practise writing the numbers and then add. Draw dots to help, if needed.

4 - - - - - - - - - - - - - - - - - -

$$\begin{array}{r} 2 \\ +5 \\ \hline \end{array}$$

$$\begin{array}{r} 3 \\ +1 \\ \hline \end{array}$$

5 - - - - - - - - - - - - - - - - - -

6 - - - - - - - - - - - - - - - - - -

7 - - - - - - - - - - - - - - - - - -

$$\begin{array}{r} 4 \\ +1 \\ \hline \end{array}$$

$$\begin{array}{r} 2 \\ +4 \\ \hline \end{array}$$

Addition 6, 7, 8

Directions: Practise writing the numbers and then add. Draw dots to help, if needed.

6 - - - - - - - - - - - - - - - -

7 - - - - - - - - - - - - - - - -

8 - - - - - - - - - - - - - - - -

$$\begin{array}{r} 3 \\ +4 \\ \hline \end{array}$$

$$\begin{array}{r} 5 \\ +1 \\ \hline \end{array}$$

$$\begin{array}{r} 2 \\ +6 \\ \hline \end{array}$$

$$\begin{array}{r} 4 \\ +4 \\ \hline \end{array}$$

Addition 7, 8, 9

Directions: Practise writing the numbers and then add. Draw dots to help, if needed.

7 - - - - - - - - - - - - - - - - - -

8 - - - - - - - - - - - - - - - - - -

9 - - - - - - - - - - - - - - - - - -

$$\begin{array}{r} 8 \\ +1 \\ \hline \end{array} \qquad \begin{array}{r} 3 \\ +5 \\ \hline \end{array}$$

$$\begin{array}{r} 2 \\ +7 \\ \hline \end{array} \qquad \begin{array}{r} 6 \\ +1 \\ \hline \end{array}$$

Name _____

Addition Table

Directions: Add across and down with a friend. Fill in the spaces.

+	0	1	2	3	4	5
0	0					
1	1	2				
2			4			
3	3			6		
4						
5						10

Do you notice any number patterns in the Addition Table?

217

Name _____

Subtraction 1, 2, 3

Subtraction means "taking away" or subtracting one number from another. "–" is a minus sign. It means to subtract the second number from the first.

Directions: Practise writing the numbers and then subtract. Draw dots and cross them out, if needed.

1

2

3

$$\begin{array}{r} 3 \\ -1 \\ \hline 2 \end{array}$$

$$\begin{array}{r} 4 \\ -3 \\ \hline \end{array}$$

$$\begin{array}{r} 2 \\ -1 \\ \hline \end{array}$$

$$\begin{array}{r} 3 \\ -2 \\ \hline \end{array}$$

Name _____

Subtraction 3, 4, 5, 6

Directions: Practise writing the numbers and then subtract.
Draw dots and cross them out, if needed.

3   - - - - - - - - - - - - - - - - -

         5   6

4   - - - - - - - - - - - - - - - - -

      -2   -1

5   - - - - - - - - - - - - - - - - -

6   - - - - - - - - - - - - - - - - -

         6   5

      -3   -1

Name _____

Subtraction

Directions: Draw the correct number of dots next to the numbers in each problem. Cross out the ones subtracted to find your answer.

Example:

$$5 \quad \bullet\bullet\bullet\bullet$$
$$\underline{-2} \quad \text{✗✗}$$
$$3$$

$$2 - 1 = 1$$
$$\bullet \qquad \text{✗}$$

$4 - 2 = \underline{}$	8 $\underline{-6}$
6 $\underline{-1}$	$3 - 1 = \underline{}$
$9 - 6 = \underline{}$	4 $\underline{-3}$

Name _____

Review

Directions: Trace the numbers. Work the problems.

9	6	3	2
-3	+2	+4	-1

5	9	7	8
+4	-5	+2	-6

4	6	9	1
-2	+3	-7	+7

Name _____

Zero

Directions: Write the number.

Example:

How many monkeys?

3

How many monkeys?

0

How many kites?

How many kites?

How many flowers?

How many flowers?

How many apples?

How many apples?

Name _____

Zero

Directions: Write the number that tells how many.

How many sailboats?

_ _ _ _ _ _ _ _ _ _ _ _ _ _ _

How many sailboats?

_ _ _ _ _ _ _ _ _ _ _ _ _ _ _

How many eggs?

_ _ _ _ _ _ _ _ _ _ _ _ _ _ _

How many eggs?

_ _ _ _ _ _ _ _ _ _ _ _ _ _ _

How many marshmallows?

_ _ _ _ _ _ _ _ _ _ _ _ _ _ _

How many marshmallows?

_ _ _ _ _ _ _ _ _ _ _ _ _ _ _

How many candles?

_ _ _ _ _ _ _ _ _ _ _ _ _ _ _

How many candles?

_ _ _ _ _ _ _ _ _ _ _ _ _ _ _

Name _____

Picture Problems: Addition

Directions: Solve the number problem under each picture.

6 + 2 = _____

3 + 1 = _____

5 + 3 = _____

1 + 7 = _____

4 + 5 = _____

+

0 + 7 = _____

Name _____

Picture Problems: Addition

Directions: Solve the number problem under each picture.

1 + 3 = _____

2 + 4 = _____

3 + 5 = _____

6 + 2 = _____

8 + 1 = _____

0 + 7 = _____

Name _____

Picture Problems: Subtraction

Directions: Solve the number problem under each picture.

5 - 2 = ____

6 - 1 = ____

7 - 4 = ____

8 - 3 = ____

9 - 2 = ____

4 - 4 = ____

Picture Problems: Subtraction

Directions: Solve the number problem under each picture.

$$6 - 2 = \rule{1cm}{0.15mm}$$

$$9 - 5 = \rule{1cm}{0.15mm}$$

$$7 - 2 = \rule{1cm}{0.15mm}$$

$$4 - 1 = \rule{1cm}{0.15mm}$$

$$8 - 1 = \rule{1cm}{0.15mm}$$

$$4 - 0 = \rule{1cm}{0.15mm}$$

Name _____

Picture Problems: Addition and Subtraction

Directions: Solve the number problem under each picture.

7 - 4 = _____

1 + 4 = _____

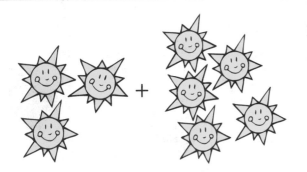

3 + 5 = _____

8 - 1 = _____

9 + 5 = _____

6 - 3 = _____

Picture Problems: Addition and Subtraction

Directions: Solve the number problem under each picture.
Write **+** or **−** to show if you should add or subtract.

How many s in all?

4 + 5 = _____

How many s in all?

7   5 = _____

How many s are left?
12   3 = _____

How many s are left?
15   8 = _____

How many s in all?
5   8 = _____

How many s are left?
11   4 = _____

Name _____

Picture Problems: Addition and Subtraction

Directions: Solve the number problem under each picture.
Write **+** or **–** to show if you should add or subtract.

How many s in all?

7 + 5 = ___12___

How many s are left?

8 ___ 3 = _____

How many s are left?

9 ___ 4 = _____

How many s in all?

14 ___ 1 = _____

How many ✏s are left?

15 ___ 6 = _____

How many s in all?

9 ___ 5 = _____

Name _____

Review: Addition and Subtraction

Directions: Solve the number problem under each picture.
Write **+** or **–** to show if you should add or subtract.

How many s are left?

12　　**4** = _____

How many s in all?

6　　**8** = _____

How many s are left?

4　　**4** = _____

How many s are left?

11　　**7** = _____

How many s in all?

9　　**3** = _____

How many s in all?

10　　**0** = _____

Name _____

Addition 1-5

Directions: Count the tools in each tool box. Write your answers in the blanks. Circle the problem that matches your answer.

4
___

(2
+2)

2
+1

___

5
+0

4
+2

___

6
+2

4
+3

___

3
+1

2
+3

Name _____

Addition 1-5

Directions: Look at the red numbers and draw that many more flowers in the pot. Count them to get your total.

Example: 3 + 2 = _5_

1 + 4 = ___

$$\begin{array}{r} 1 \\ +1 \\ \hline \end{array}$$

$$\begin{array}{r} 2 \\ +2 \\ \hline \end{array}$$

3 + 1 = ___

Name _____

Addition 1-5

Directions: Add the numbers. Put your answers in the nests.

Example: $2 + 3 = $ 5

$1 + 2 = $

$1 + 3 = $

$4 + 1 = $

$1 + 1 = $

Addition 6-10

Directions: Add the numbers. Put your answers in the doghouses.

Example: $4 + 2 =$ 6

$2 + 6 =$

$7 + 3 =$

$6 + 1 =$

$4 + 5 =$

$6 + 2 =$

$7 + 2 =$

Name _____

Subtraction 1-5

Directions: Subtract the red numbers by crossing out that many flowers in the pot. Count the ones not crossed out to get the total.

Example:

$2 - 1 = \underline{1}$

$5 - 2 = \underline{\hphantom{0}}$

$$4$$
$$\underline{-2}$$

$$3$$
$$\underline{-1}$$

$4 - 3 = \underline{\hphantom{0}}$

Name _____

Subtraction 1-5

Directions: Count the fruit in each bowl. Write your answers on the blanks. Circle the problem that matches your answer.

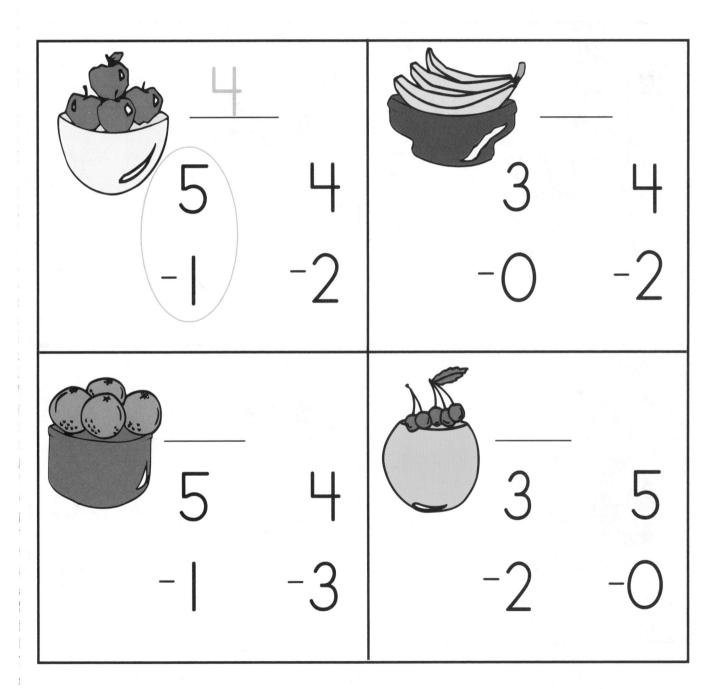

Name _____

Subtraction 6-10

Directions: Count the flowers. Write your answer on the blank. Circle the problem that matches your answer.

_____

$$10 \qquad 9$$
$$-1 \qquad -1$$

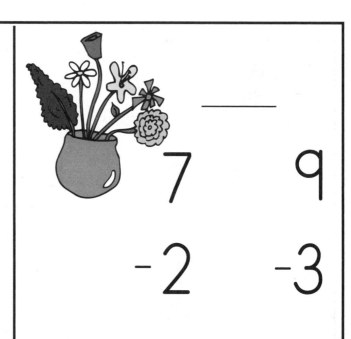

_____

$$7 \qquad 9$$
$$-2 \qquad -3$$

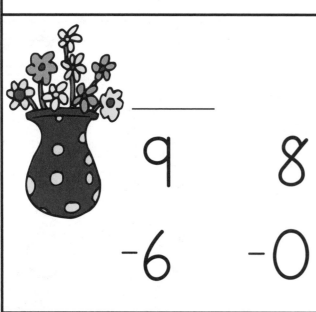

_____

$$9 \qquad 8$$
$$-6 \qquad -0$$

_____

$$10 \qquad 8$$
$$-2 \qquad -1$$

Name _____

Addition and Subtraction

Directions: Solve the problems. Remember, addition means "putting together" or adding two or more numbers to find the sum. Subtraction means "taking away" or subtracting one number from another.

$1 + 3 =$ _____ $4 - 3 =$ _____ $4 + 5 =$ _____

$6 + 1 =$ _____ $7 - 2 =$ _____ $8 - 4 =$ _____

$9 - 1 =$ _____ $10 - 3 =$ _____

$5 - 2 =$ _____ $6 + 3 =$ _____

$8 + 2 =$ _____ $5 + 5 =$ _____

Name _____

Addition and Subtraction

Remember, addition means "putting together" or adding two or more numbers to find the sum. Subtraction means "take away" or subtracting one number from another.

Directions: Solve the problems. From your answers, use the code to colour the quilt.

Colour:
- 6 = blue
- 7 = yellow
- 8 = green
- 9 = red
- 10 = orange

$$6 + 3$$

$$9 + 1$$

$$12 - 6 =$$

$$10 - 2 =$$

$$10 - 4$$

$$4 + 6$$

$$11 - 2$$

$$5 + 5$$

$$12 - 6$$

$$10 - 1$$

$$3 + 4$$

$$12 - 5$$

$$10 - 3$$

$$6 + 1$$

$$11 - 5$$

$$3 + 5$$

$$11 - 1$$

$$4 + 4$$

$$6 + 2$$

$$6 + 3$$

$$1 + 5 =$$

$$9 - 2 =$$

$$6 + 2 =$$

Name _____

Place Value: Tens and Ones

The place value of a digit, or numeral, is shown by where it is in the number. For example, in the number **23**, **2** has the place value of **tens**, and **3** is ones.

Directions: Count the groups of ten crayons and write the number by the word **tens**. Count the other crayons and write the number by the word **ones**.

Example: + = _|_ ten + _|_ one

 + = ____ tens + ____ ones

  + = ____ tens + ____ ones

 + = ____ tens + ____ ones

---

6 tens + 3 ones = ____   5 tens + 1 one = ____

3 tens + 8 ones = ____   9 tens + 7 ones = ____

4 tens + 5 ones = ____   2 tens + 8 ones = ____

Name _____

Place Value: Tens and Ones

Directions: Count the groups of ten blocks and write the number by the word tens. Count the other blocks and write the number by the word ones.

Example:

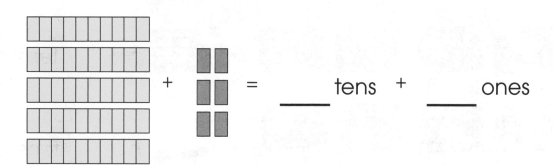

[blocks] + [blocks] = __1__ ten + __2__ ones

[blocks] + [blocks] = _____ tens + _____ ones

[blocks] + [blocks] = _____ tens + _____ ones

[blocks] + [blocks] = _____ tens + _____ ones

[blocks] + [blocks] = _____ tens + _____ ones

Name _____

Place Value: Tens and Ones

Directions: Write the answers in the correct spaces.

		tens	ones		
3 tens, 2 ones		_3_	_2_	=	_32_
3 tens, 7 ones		____	____	=	____
9 tens, 1 one		____	____	=	____
5 tens, 6 ones		____	____	=	____
6 tens, 5 ones		____	____	=	____
6 tens, 8 ones		____	____	=	____
2 tens, 8 ones		____	____	=	____
4 tens, 9 ones		____	____	=	____
1 ten, 4 ones		____	____	=	____
8 tens, 2 ones		____	____	=	____
4 tens, 2 ones		____	____	=	____

28 = ____ tens, ____ ones

64 = ____ tens, ____ ones

56 = ____ tens, ____ ones

72 = ____ tens, ____ ones

38 = ____ tens, ____ ones

17 = ____ ten, ____ ones

63 = ____ tens, ____ ones

12 = ____ ten, ____ ones

Review: Place Value

The place value of each digit, or numeral, is shown by where it is in the number. For example, in the number **123**, **1** has the place value of **hundreds**, **2** is **tens** and **3** is **ones**.

Directions: Count the groups of crayons and add.

Example:

 + + =

	Hundreds	Tens	Ones
	1	1	3

1 Hundred + **1 Ten** + **3 Ones**

 + + = ____ ____ ____

 + + = ____ ____ ____

Counting by Fives

Directions: Count by fives to draw the path to the playground.

Name _____

Counting by Fives

Directions: Use tally marks to count by fives. Write the number next to the tallies.

Example: A tally mark stands for one = I. Five tally marks look like this = ⑪

卌	_____	卌 卌 卌 卌 卌 卌 卌	_____
卌 卌	_____	卌 卌 卌 卌 卌 卌 卌 卌	_____
卌 卌 卌	_____	卌 卌 卌 卌 卌 卌	_____
卌 卌 卌 卌	_____	卌 卌 卌 卌 卌 卌 卌 卌 卌	_____
卌 卌 卌 卌 卌	_____	卌 卌 卌 卌 卌 卌 卌 卌 卌 卌	_____
卌 卌 卌 卌 卌 卌	_____		

246

Counting by Tens

Directions: Count in order by tens to draw the path the boy takes to the store.

Name _____

Counting by Tens

Directions: Use the groups of 10's to count to 100.

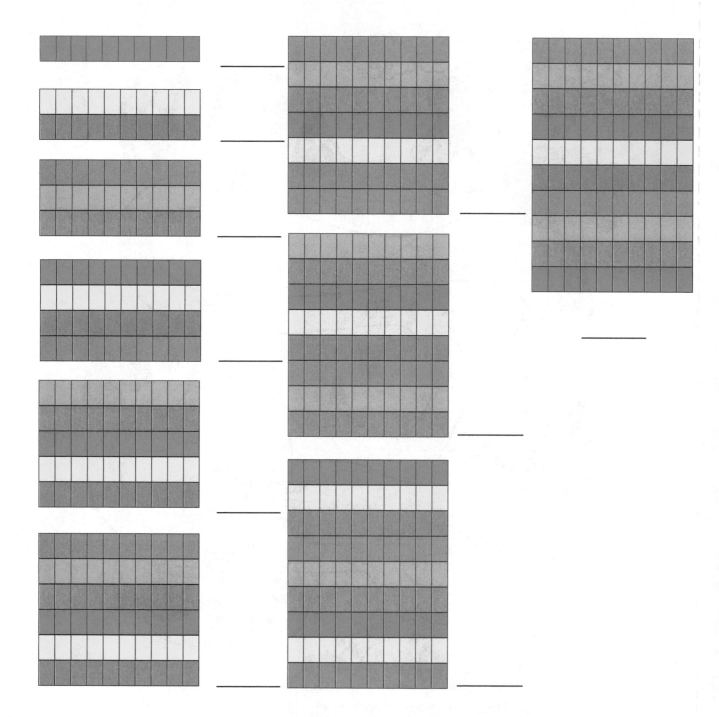

248

Name _____

Addition: 10-15

Directions: Circle groups of ten crayons. Add the remaining ones to make the correct number.

		tens	ones
	+ =	3	9
	+ =		
	+ =		
	+ =		
	+ =		
	+ =		

6 + 6 = ____   8 + 4 = ____   9 + 5 = ____

Name _____

Subtraction: 10-15

Directions: Count the crayons in each group. Put an **X** through the number of crayons being subtracted. How many are left?

		-	5	=	10
		-	4	=	____
		-	7	=	____
		-	6	=	____
		-	5	=	____
		-	8	=	____

13 - 8 = _____   11 - 5 = _____   12 - 9 = _____

14 - 7 = _____   10 - 7 = _____   13 - 3 = _____

15 - 9 = _____   11 - 8 = _____   12 - 10 = _____

Shapes: Square

A square is a figure with four corners and four sides of the same length. This is a square ☐.

Directions: Find the squares and circle them.

Directions: Trace the word. Write the word.

square

Shapes: Circle

A circle is a figure that is round. This is a circle ○.

Directions: Find the circles and put a square around them.

Directions: Trace the word. Write the word.

Shapes: Square and Circle

Directions: Practise drawing squares. Trace the samples and make four of your own.

Directions: Practise drawing circles. Trace the samples and make four of your own.

Shapes: Triangle

A triangle is a figure with three corners and three sides. This is a triangle △.

Directions: Find the triangles and put a circle around them.

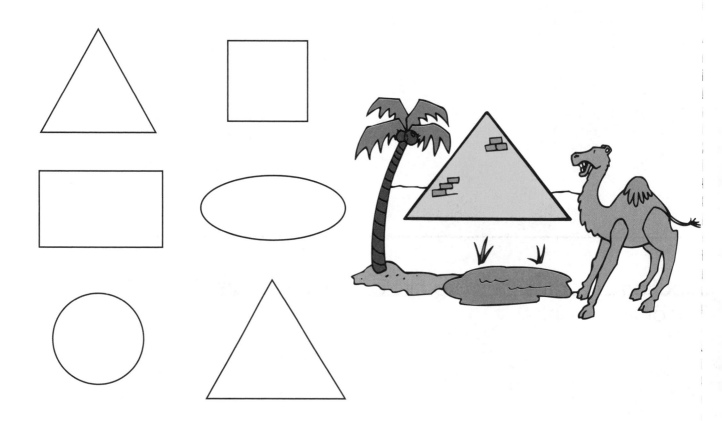

Directions: Trace the word. Write the word.

Name _____

Shapes: Rectangle

A rectangle is a figure with four corners and four sides. Sides opposite each other are the same length. This is a rectangle ▭ .

Directions: Find the rectangles and put a circle around them.

Directions: Trace the word. Write the word.

rectangle

_____

Name _____

Shapes: Triangle and Rectangle

Directions: Practise drawing triangles. Trace the samples and make four of your own.

Directions: Practise drawing rectangles. Trace the samples and make four of your own.

Patterns: Rectangles

Directions: In each picture, there is more than one rectangle. Trace each rectangle with a different colour crayon. Under each picture, write how many rectangles you found.

_____ rectangles

_____ rectangles

Name _____

Patterns: Triangles

Directions: In each picture there is more than one triangle. Trace each triangle with a different colour crayon. Under each picture, write how many triangles you found.

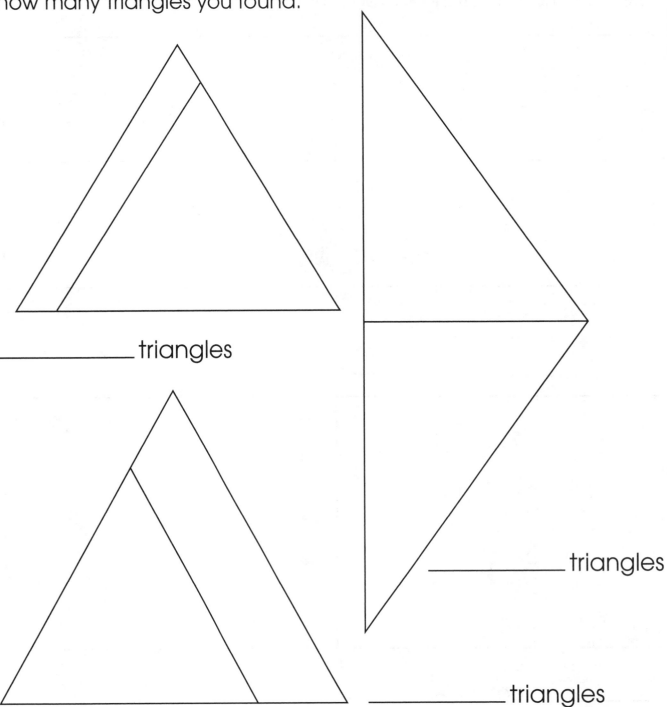

_____ triangles

_____ triangles

_____ triangles

Shapes: Oval and Rhombus

An oval is an egg-shaped figure. A rhombus is a figure with four sides of the same length. Its corners form points at the top, sides and bottom. This is an oval ⬭. This is a rhombus ◇.

Directions: Colour the ovals red. Colour the rhombuses blue.

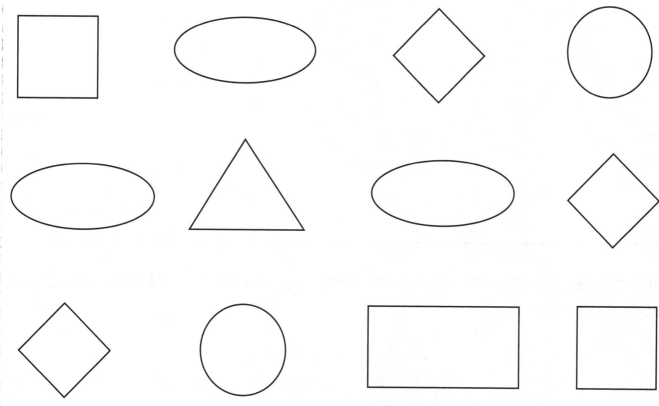

Directions: Trace the words. Write the words.

oval

rhombus

Shapes: Oval and Rhombus

Directions: Practise drawing ovals. Trace the samples and make four of your own.

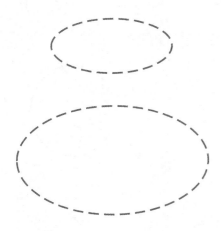

Directions: Practise drawing rhombuses. Trace the samples and mak four of your own.

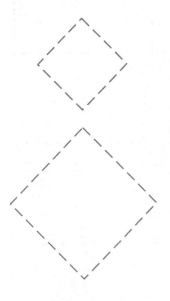

Name _____

Following Directions: Shapes and Colours

Directions: Colour the squares ☐ purple.

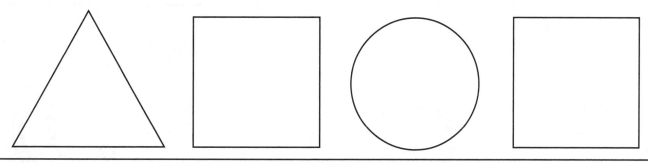

Directions: Colour the heart ♡ blue.

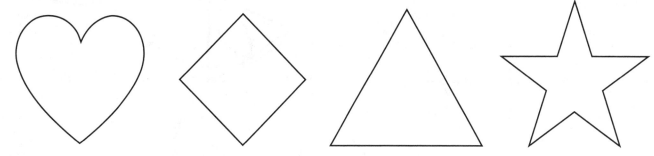

Directions: Colour the rhombuses ◇ yellow.

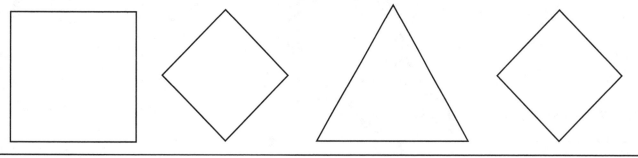

Directions: Colour the star ☆ red.

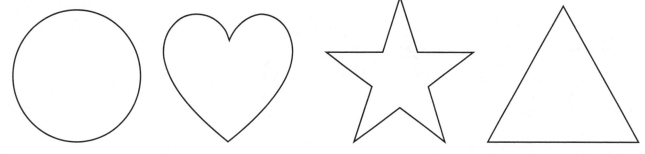

Math   261   Complete Early Skills Grade 1

Shape Review

Directions: Colour the shapes in the picture as shown.

black

red

orange

yellow

blue

green

Shape Review

Directions: Trace the circles
Trace the squares
Trace the rectangles
Trace the triangles
Trace the ovals
Trace the rhombuses

Name _____

Classifying: Stars

Help Bob find the stars.

Directions: Colour all the stars blue.

How many stars did you and Bob find?_____

Name _____

Classifying: Shapes

Mary and Rudy are taking a trip into space. Help them find the stars, moons, circles and rhombuses.

Directions: Colour the shapes.

Use yellow for ☆'s.   Use blue for ☾'s.

Use red for O's.   Use purple for ◇'s.

How many stars?_____   How many moons?_____

How many circles?_____   How many rhombuses?_____

Name _____

Classifying: Shapes

Directions: Look at the shapes. Answer the questions.

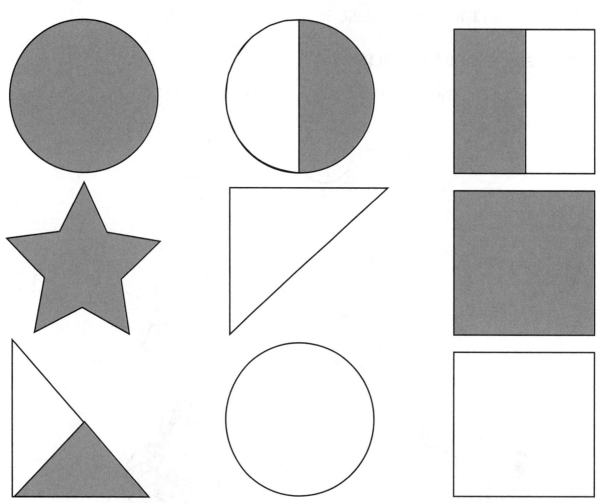

1. How many all-white shapes? _____

2. How many all-blue shapes? _____

3. How many half-white shapes? _____

4. How many all-blue stars? _____

5. How many all-white circles? _____

6. How many half-blue shapes? _____

Name _____

Same and Different: Shapes

Directions: Colour the shape that looks the same as the first shape in each row.

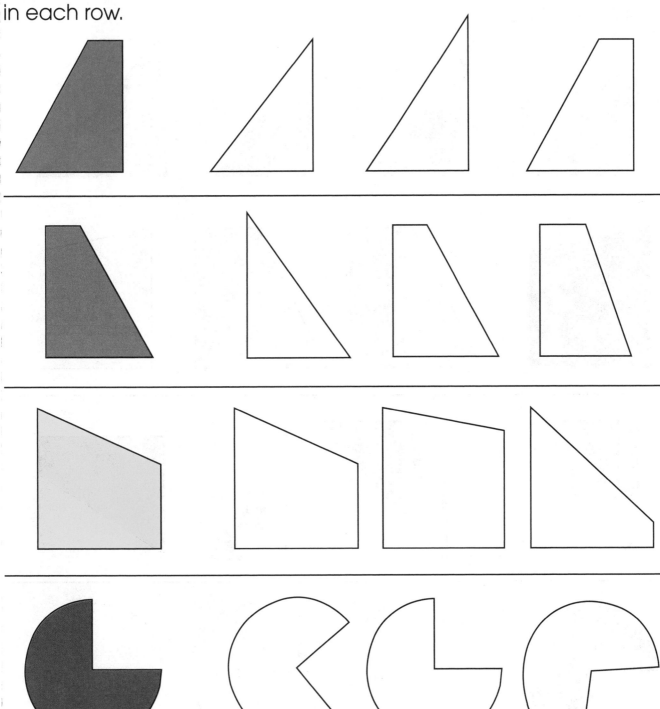

267

Name _____

Same and Different: Shapes

Directions: Draw an **X** on the shapes in each row that do not match the first shape.

268

Name _____

Copying: Shapes and Colours

Directions: Colour your circle to look the same.

Directions: Colour your square to look the same.

Directions: Trace the triangle. Colour it to look the same.

Directions: Trace the star. Colour it to look the same.

Copying: Shapes and Colours

Directions: Colour the second shape the same as the first one. Then draw and colour the shape two more times.

Patterns: Shapes

Directions: Draw a line from the box on the left to the box on the right with the same shape and colour pattern.

Name _____

Patterns: Shapes

Directions: Draw a line from the box on the left to the box on the right with the same shape and colour pattern.

Patterns: Find and Copy

Directions: Circle the shape in the middle box that matches the one on the left. Draw another shape with the same pattern in the box on the right.

Math

273

Complete Early Skills Grade 1

Name _____

Patterns

Directions: Draw what comes next in each pattern.

Example:

274

Name _____

Patterns

Directions: Fill in the missing shape in each row. Then colour it.

_____

_____

_____

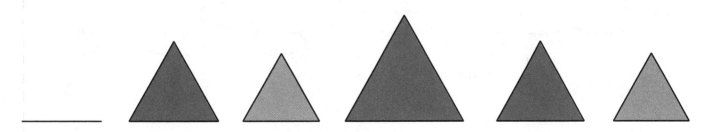

Name _____

Patterns

Directions: Colour to complete the patterns.

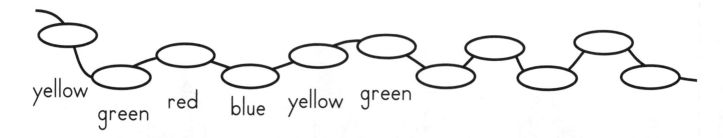

276

Fractions: Whole and Half

A fraction is a number that names part of a whole, such as $\frac{1}{2}$ or $\frac{3}{4}$.

Directions: Colour half of each object.

Example:

Whole apple

Half an apple

$$\frac{1}{2}$$

Name _____

Fractions: Halves $\frac{1}{2}$

$\frac{1}{2}$ $\dfrac{\text{Part shaded or divided}}{\text{Number of equal parts}}$

Directions: Colour only the shapes that show halves.

278

Name _____

Fractions: Thirds $\frac{1}{3}$

Directions: Circle the objects that have 3 equal parts.

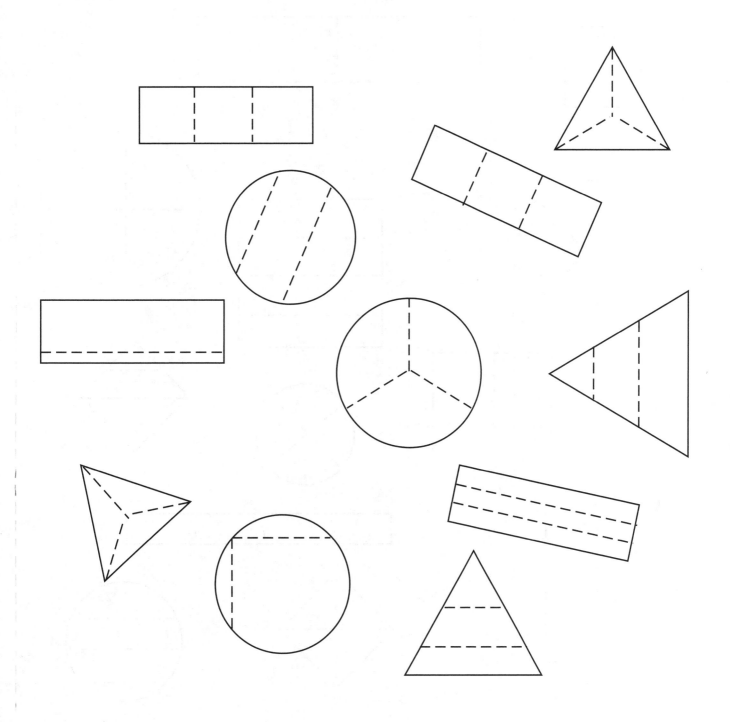

Name _____

Fractions: Fourths $\frac{1}{4}$

Directions: Circle the objects that have four equal parts.

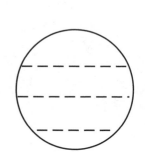

Name _____

Fractions: Thirds and Fourths

Directions: Each object has 3 equal parts. Colour one section.

  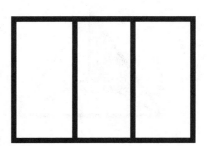

Directions: Each object has 4 equal parts. Colour one section.

281

Name _____

Review: Fractions

Directions: Count the equal parts, then write the fraction.

Example:

Shaded part = __1__   Write

Equal parts = __3__ $\dfrac{1}{3}$

Shaded part = __1__   Write

Equal parts = ____   ___

Shaded part = __1__   Write

Equal parts = ____   ___

Shaded part = __1__   Write

Equal parts = ____   ___

Review

Directions: Write the missing numbers by counting by tens and fives.

_____ , 20, _____ , _____ , _____ , _____ , 70, _____ , _____ , 100

5, _____ , 15, _____ , _____ , 30, _____ , _____ , _____ , _____

Directions: Colour the object with thirds red. Colour the object with halves blue. Colour the object with fourths green.

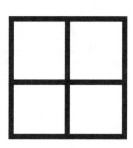

Directions: Draw a line to the correct equal part.

$\dfrac{1}{3}$

$\dfrac{1}{4}$

$\dfrac{1}{2}$

Name _____

Tracking: Straight Lines

Directions: Draw a straight line from A to B. Use a different colour crayon for each line.

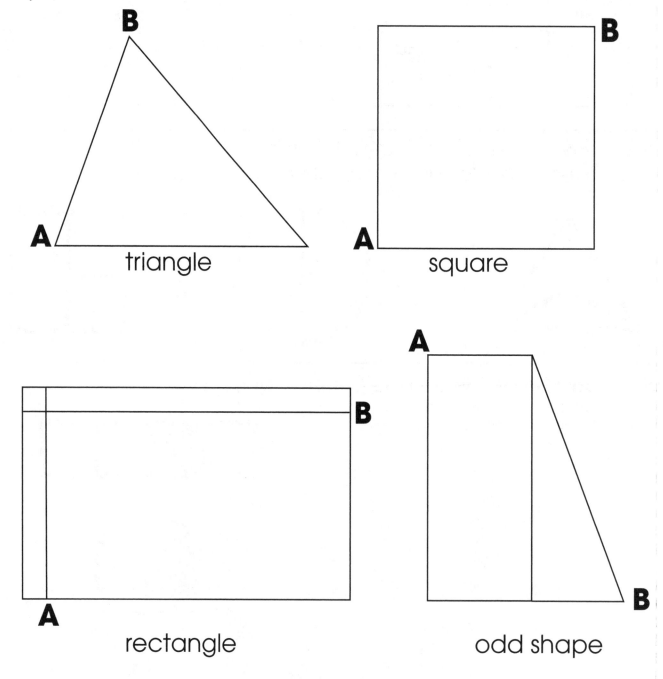

triangle

square

rectangle

odd shape

What shapes do you see hidden in these shapes?

Tracking: Different Paths

Directions: Trace three paths from A to B.

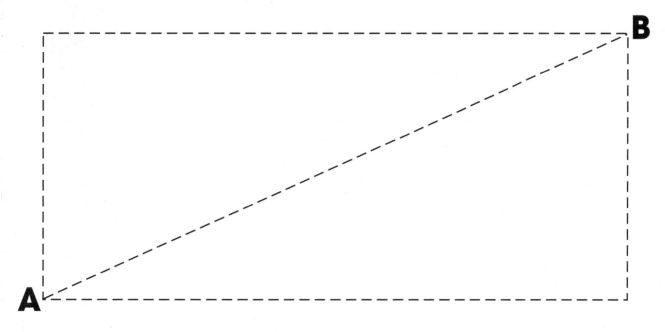

Directions: Trace the path from A to B.

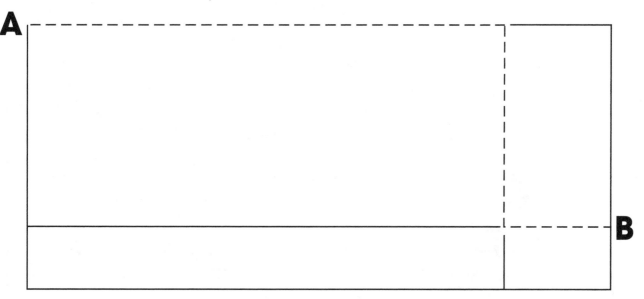

How many corners did you turn?_____

Tracking: Different Paths

Help Megan find Mark.

Directions: Trace a path from Megan to Mark.

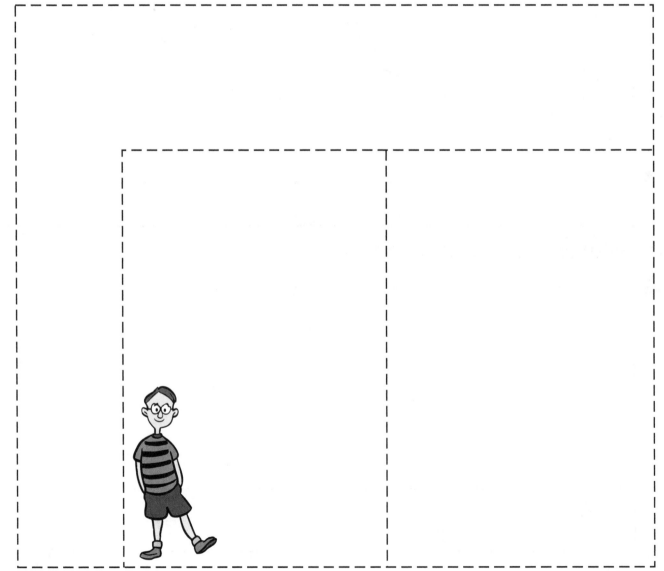

How many different paths can she follow to reach him? _____

Name _____

Tracking: Different Paths

Directions: Use different colours to trace three paths the bear could take to get the honey.

Name _____

Time: Hour

The short hand of the clock tells the hour. The long hand tells how many minutes after the hour. When the minute hand is on the **12**, it is the beginning of the hour.

Directions: Look at each clock. Write the time.

Example:

_3_ o'clock

____ o'clock

____ o'clock

____ o'clock

____ o'clock

____ o'clock

____ o'clock

____ o'clock

____ o'clock

Name _____

Time: Hour, Half-Hour

The short hand of the clock tells the hour. The long hand tells how many minutes after the hour. When the minute hand is on the **6**, it is on the half-hour. A half-hour is thirty minutes. It is written **:30**, such as **5:30**.

Directions: Look at each clock. Write the time.

Example:

hour   half-hour

_1_ : _30_

___ : ___   ___ : ___   ___ : ___   ___ : ___

___ : ___   ___ : ___   ___ : ___   ___ : ___

Name _____

Time: Hour, Half-Hour

Directions: Draw the hands on each clock to show the correct time.

 2:30

 9:00

 7:00

 4:30

 3:00

 1:30

Name _____

Time: Counting by Fives

Directions: Fill in the numbers on the clock face. Count by fives around the clock.

There are 60 minutes in one hour.

Time: Review

Directions: Look at the time on the digital clocks and draw the hands on the clocks.

Directions: Look at each clock. Write the time.

 _____o'clock   _____o'clock

Directions: Look at each clock. Write the time.

___:___   ___:___   ___:___

Name _____

Review: Time

Directions: Tell what time it is on the clocks.

 _____

 _____

 _____

 _____

 _____

 _____

Name _____

Review: Time

Directions: Match the time on the clock with the digital time.

| 10:00 |

| 5:00 |

| 3:00 |

| 9:00 |

| 2:00 |

Name _____

Money: Penny and Nickel

A penny is worth one cent. It is written **1¢** or **$.01**. A nickel is worth five cents. It is written **5¢** or **$.05**.

Directions: Count the money and write the answers.

penny   1 penny = 1¢

nickel   1 nickel = 5¢

= __3__ ¢

= __15__ ¢

= _____ ¢

= _____ ¢

= _____ ¢

= _____ ¢

Name _____

Money: Penny, Nickel, Dime

A penny is worth one cent. It is written **1¢** or **$.01**. A nickel is worth five cents. It is written **5¢** or **$.05**. A dime is worth ten cents. It is written **10¢** or **$.10**.

Directions: Add the coins pictured and write the total amounts in the blanks.

Example:

dime		**nickel**		**nickel**		**pennies**
10¢	=	5¢	+	5¢	=	10¢

10¢ + 1¢ = _____ ¢   10¢ + _____ ¢ = _____ ¢

_____ ¢ + _____ ¢ + _____ ¢ = _____ ¢

_____ ¢ + _____ ¢ = _____ ¢

Name _____

Money

Directions: Match the amounts in each purse to the price tags.

Name _____

Money: Penny, Nickel, Dime

Directions: Match the correct amount of money with the price of the object.

Review: Money

Directions: What time is it?

_____ o'clock

Directions: Draw the hands on each clock.

2:30

7:30

11:00

Directions: How much money?

= _____ ¢   = _____ ¢

Directions: Add or subtract.

9 + 3 = _____   6 + 8 = _____   15 - 9 = _____

12 - 8 = _____   12 + 2 = _____   7 + 6 = _____

Name _____

Review

Directions: Follow the instructions.
1. How much money?

_____ ¢

	Tens	Ones			Hundreds	Tens	Ones
2. 57 =	_____	_____	128	=	_____	_____	_____

3. What is this shape? Circle the answer.

Square
Triangle
Circle

What is this shape? _____

4.

Shaded part = _____   Write ___

Equal parts = _____

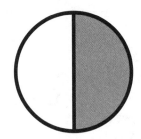

Shaded part = _____   Write ___

Equal parts = _____

5.   12 + 3 = _____   9 + 6 = _____   15 - 7 = _____

Name _____

Measurement

A ruler has 36 centimetres.

Directions: Cut out the ruler at the bottom of the page. Measure the objects to the nearest centimetre.

The screwdriver is _____ centimetres long.

The pencil is _____ centimetres long.

The pen is _____ centimetres long.

The fork is _____ centimetres long.

__Cut ✂__ _____

cm

Page is blank for cutting exercise on previous page.

Page 6

Name, Address, Phone

This book belongs to

Answers will vary.

I live at

Answers will vary.

The city I live in is

Answers will vary.

The province or territory I live in is

Answers will vary.

My phone number is

Answers will vary.

Page 7

Review the Alphabet

Directions: Practise writing the letters.

Aa
Bb
Cc
Dd
Ee
Ff
Gg
Hh
Ii

Child will write letters as shown.

Page 8

Review the Alphabet

Directions: Practise writing the letters.

Jj
Kk
Ll
Mm
Nn
Oo
Pp
Qq
Rr

Child will write letters as shown.

Page 9

Review the Alphabet

Directions: Practise writing the letters.

Ss
Tt
Uu
Vv
Ww
Xx
Yy
Zz

Child will write letters as shown.

Page 10

Letter Recognition

Directions: In each set, match the lower-case letter to the upper-case letter.

Page 11

Letter Recognition

Directions: In each set, match the lower-case letter to the upper-case letter.

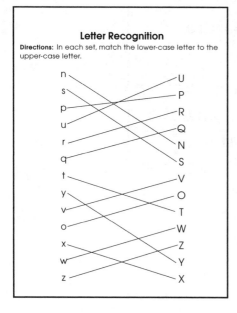

Page 12

Beginning Consonants: Bb, Cc, Dd, Ff

Beginning consonants are the sounds that come at the beginning of words. Consonants are the letters b, c, d, f, g, h, j, k, l, m, n, p, q, r, s, t, v, w, x, y and z.

Directions: Say the name of each letter. Say the sound each letter makes. Circle the letters that make the beginning sound for each picture.

Page 13

Beginning Consonants: Bb, Cc, Dd, Ff

Directions: Say the name of each letter. Say the sound each letter makes. Draw a line from each letter to the picture which begins with that sound.

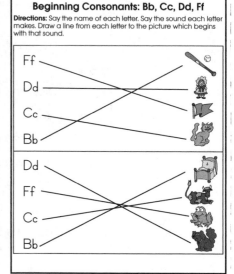

Page 14

Beginning Consonants: Gg, Hh, Jj, Kk

Directions: Say the name of each letter. Say the sound each letter makes. Trace the letter pair that makes the beginning sound in each picture.

Page 15

Beginning Consonants: Gg, Hh, Jj, Kk

Directions: Say the name of each letter. Say the sound each letter makes. Draw a line from each letter pair to the picture which begins with that sound.

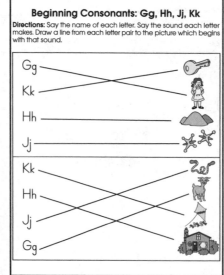

Page 16

Beginning Consonants: Ll, Mm, Nn, Pp

Directions: Say the name of each letter. Say the sound each letter makes. Trace the letters. Then draw a line from each letter pair to the picture which begins with that sound.

Page 17

Beginning Consonants: Ll, Mm, Nn, Pp

Directions: Say the name of each letter. Say the sound each letter makes. Trace the letter pair that makes the beginning sound in each picture.

Ll Mm Nn Pp

Mm **Ll**	**Mm** Pp
Ll Nn	**Pp** Mm

Page 18

Beginning Consonants: Qq, Rr, Ss, Tt

Directions: Say the name of each letter. Say the sound each letter makes. Trace the letter pair in the boxes. Then colour the picture which begins with that sound.

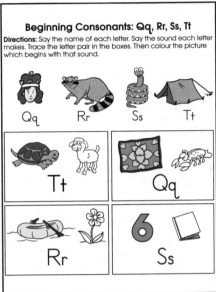

Qq Rr Ss Tt

Tt	**Qq**
Rr	**Ss**

Page 19

Beginning Consonants: Qq, Rr, Ss, Tt

Directions: Say the name of each letter. Say the sound each letter makes. Draw a line from each letter pair to the picture which begins with that sound.

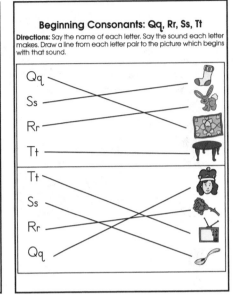

Qq
Ss
Rr
Tt

Tt
Ss
Rr
Qq

Page 20

Beginning Consonants: Vv, Ww, Xx, Yy, Zz

Directions: Say the name of each letter. Say the sound each letter makes. Trace the letters. Then draw a line from each letter pair to the picture which begins with that sound.

Vv Ww Xx Yy Zz

V v
W w
X x
Y y
Z z

Page 21

Beginning Consonants: Vv, Ww, Xx, Yy, Zz

Directions: Say the name of each letter. Say the sound each letter makes. Then draw a line from each letter pair to the picture which begins with that sound.

Vv
Zz
Xx
Yy
Ww

Vv
Zz
Yy
Ww
Xx

Page 22

Ending Consonants: b, d, f

Ending consonants are the sounds that come at the end of words.
Directions: Say the name of each picture. Then write the letter which makes the **ending** sound for each picture.

b	f	d
b	d	f
f	d	f
b	d	b

Page 23

Ending Consonants: g, m, n

Directions: Say the name of each picture. Draw a line from each letter to the pictures which end with that sound.

g   m   n

Page 24

Ending Consonants: k, l, p

Directions: Trace the letters in each row. Say the name of each picture. Then colour the pictures in each row which end with that sound.

k

l

p

Page 25

Ending Consonants: r, s, t, x

Directions: Say the name of each picture. Then circle the ending sound for each picture.

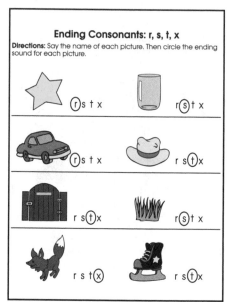

(r) s t x   r (s) t x

(r) s t x   r s (t) x

r s (t) x   (r) s t x

r s t (x)   r s (t) x

Page 26

Short Vowels

Vowels are the letters a, e, i, o and u. Short a is the sound you hear in **ant**. Short e is the sound you hear in **elephant**. Short i is the sound you hear in **igloo**. Short o is the sound you hear in **octopus**. Short u is the sound you hear in **umbrella**.

Directions: Say the short vowel sound at the beginning of each row. Say the name of each picture. Then colour the pictures which have the same short vowel sounds as that letter.

ă
ĕ
ĭ
ŏ
ŭ

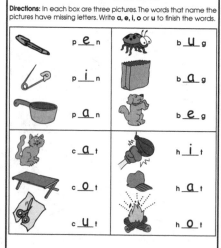

Page 27

Short Vowel Sounds

Directions: In each box are three pictures. The words that name the pictures have missing letters. Write a, e, i, o or u to finish the words.

p _e_ n   b _u_ g

p _i_ n   b _a_ g

p _a_ n   b _e_ g

c _a_ t   h _i_ t

c _o_ t   h _a_ t

c _u_ t   h _o_ t

Page 28

Long Vowels

Vowels are the letters a, e, i, o and u. Long vowel sounds say their own names. Long a is the sound you hear in **hay**. Long e is the sound you hear in **me**. Long i is the sound you hear in **pie**. Long o is the sound you hear in **no**. Long u is the sound you hear in **cute**.

Directions: Say the long vowel sound at the beginning of each row. Say the name of each picture. Colour the pictures in each row that have the same long vowel sound as that letter.

ā
ē
ī
ō
ū

Page 29

Long Vowel Sounds

Directions: Write a, e, i, o or u in each blank to finish the word. Draw a line from the word to the picture.

c a ke
r o se
k i te
f ee t
m u le

Page 30

Words With a

Directions: Each train has a group of pictures. Write the word that names the pictures. Read your rhyming words.

These trains use the short **a** sound like in the word cat:

pan   can   fan   man

rat   cat   bat   hat

These trains use the long **a** sound like in the word lake:

skate   gate   plate

rake   cake   snake

Page 31

Short and Long Aa

Directions: Say the name of each picture. If it has the short **a** sound, colour it **red**. If it has the long **a** sound, colour it **yellow**.

ă   ā

Page 32

Words with e

Directions: Short e sounds like the e in hen. Long e sounds like the e in bee. Look at the pictures. If the word has a short e sound, draw a line to the **hen** with your **red** crayon. If the word has a long e sound, draw a line to the **bee** with your **green** crayon.

hen   bee

Page 33

Short and Long Ee

Directions: Say the name of each picture. Circle the pictures which have the short **e** sound. Draw a triangle around the pictures which have the long **e** sound.

ĕ   ē

Page 34

Words with i

Directions: Short i sounds like the i in pig. Long i sounds like the i in kite. Draw a circle around the words with the short i sound. Draw an **X** on the words with the long i sound.

pin   five   pig
slide   kite   lid
tie   bib   pie

Page 35

Short and Long Ii

Directions: Say the name of each picture. If it has the short **i** sound, colour it **yellow**. If it has the long **i** sound, colour it **red**.

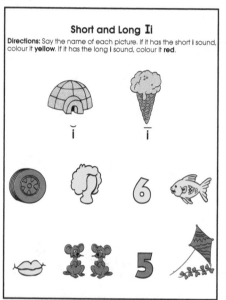

ĭ   ī

Page 36

Words With o

Directions: The short **o** sounds like the **o** in dog. Long **o** sounds like the **o** in rope. Draw a line from the picture to the word that names it. Draw a circle around the word if it has a short **o** sound.

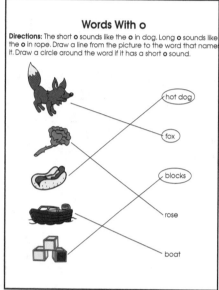

hot dog
fox
blocks
rose
boat

Page 37

Short and Long Oo

Directions: Say the name of each picture. If the picture has the long **o** sound, write a **green L** on the blank. If the picture has the short **o** sound, write a **red S** on the blank.

L   S
S   S   L
S   L

Page 38

Words With u

Directions: The short **u** sounds like the **u** in bug. The long **u** sounds like the **u** in blue. Draw a circle around the words with short **u**. Draw an **X** on the words with long **u**.

rug   cup   music
tub   suit   glue
bug   puppy   gum

Page 39

Short and Long Uu

Directions: Say the name of each picture. If it has the long **u** sound, write a **u** in the **unicorn** column. If it has the short **u** sound, write a **u** in the **umbrella** column.

ū   ŭ
_____   u
u   _____
_____   u
u   _____
_____   u

Page 40

Super Silent E

When you add an **e** to the end of some words, the vowel changes from a short vowel sound to a long vowel sound.
The **e** is silent.
Example: rip + **e** = ripe.

Directions: Say the word under the first picture in each pair. Then add an **e** to the word under the next picture. Say the new word.

pet   Pete   tub   tube
man   mane   kit   kite
pin   pine   cap   cape

Page 41

Consonant Blends

Consonant blends are two or more consonant sounds together in a word. The blend is made by combining the consonant sounds.

Example: <u>fl</u>oor

Directions: The name of each picture begins with a **blend**. Circle the beginning blend for each picture.

Page 42

Consonant Blends

Directions: The beginning blend for each word is missing. Fill in the correct blend to finish the word. Draw a line from the word to the picture.

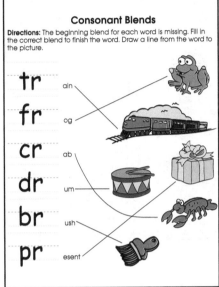

tr   ain
fr   og
cr   ab
dr   um
br   ush
pr   esent

Page 43

Consonant Blends

Directions: Draw a line from the picture to the blend that begins its word.

sk
sl
sm
sn
sp
st
sw

Page 44

Consonant Blends

Directions: Look at the first picture in each row. Circle the pictures in the row that begin with the same sound.

chair
shell
thumb
wheel

Page 45

Beginning Blends

Directions: Say the blend for each word as you search for it.

Words to find:
block	sled	globe	crab
clock	frog	present	flower
train	glove	skunk	snake
swan	flag	smell	spider
bread	small	chair	shell
stop	sled	shoe	
thumb	wheel	clown	

Page 46

Ending Consonant Blends

Directions: Write **lt** or **ft** to complete the words.

be   lt
ra   ft
sa   lt
qui   lt
le   ft

Page 47

Ending Consonant Blends

Directions: Draw a line from the picture to the blend that ends the word.

lf

lk

sk

st

Page 48

Ending Consonant Blends

Directions: Every juke box has a word ending and a list of letters. Add each of the letters to the word ending to make rhyming words.

b **and**
h **and**
l **and**
s **and**

b **ent**
d **ent**
t **ent**
w **ent**

b **ump**
d **ump**
j **ump**
p **ump**

p **ink**
s **ink**
l **ink**
th **ink**

r **ing**
s **ing**
st **ing**
k **ing**

b **ank**
r **ank**
s **ank**
t **ank**

Page 49

Ending Consonant Blends

Directions: Say the blend for each word as you search for it.

Words to find:

belt	raft	milk	shelf
mask	clasp	nest	band
think	went	lump	crank
ring	blank	shrink	land
bring	tent	dump	sing

Page 50

Rhyming Words

Rhyming words are words that sound alike at the end of the word. **Cat** and **hat** rhyme.

Directions: Draw a circle around each word pair that rhymes. Draw an **X** on each pair that does not rhyme.

Example:

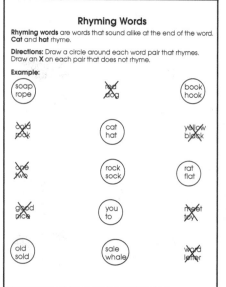

Page 51

Rhyming Words

Rhyming words are words that sound alike at the end of the word.

Directions: Draw a line to match the pictures that rhyme. Write two of your own rhyming word pairs below.

Answers will vary.

Page 52

ABC Order

Directions: Abc

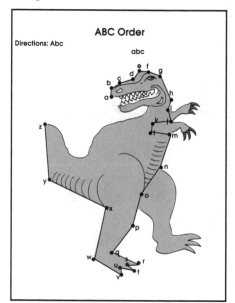

Complete Early Skills Grade 1   310   Answer Key

Page 53

ABC Order

Directions: Draw a line to connect the dots. Follow the letters in abc order. Then colour the picture.

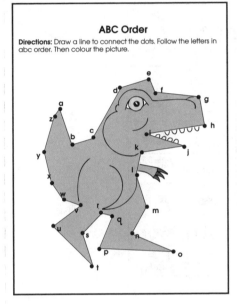

Page 54

ABC Order

Directions: Circle the first letter of each word. Then put each pair of the words in abc order.

| ⓒar | ⓑird | ⓜoon | ⓣwo | ⓝest | ⓕan |

bird   moon   fan

car   two   nest

| ⓒard | ⓓog | ⓟig | ⓑike | ⓢun | ⓟie |

card   bike   pie

dog   pig   sun

Page 55

ABC Order

Directions: Look at the words in each box. Circle the word that comes first in abc order.

(duck) four rock	chair (apple) yellow	(peach) this walk
game (boy) pink	light (come) one	(mouse) ten orange
(angel) table hair	zebra watch (five)	foot (boat) mine
look (blue) rope	who dog (black)	(book) tan six

Page 56

Compound Words

Compound words are two words that are put together to make one new word.

Directions: Look at the pictures and the two words that are next to each other. Put the words together to make a new word. Write the new word.

Example:

house + boat = **houseboat**

side + walk = **sidewalk**

lip + stick = **lipstick**

sand + box = **sandbox**

lunch + box = **lunchbox**

Page 57

Compound Words

Directions: Circle the compound word which completes each sentence. Write each word on the lines.

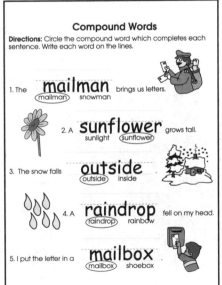

1. The **mailman** brings us letters.
   (mailman) snowman

2. A **sunflower** grows tall.
   sunlight (sunflower)

3. The snow falls **outside**.
   (outside) inside

4. A **raindrop** fell on my head.
   (raindrop) rainbow

5. I put the letter in a **mailbox**.
   (mailbox) shoebox

Page 58

Names

You are a special person. Your name begins with a capital letter. We put a capital letter at the beginning of people's names because they are special.

Directions: Write your name. Did you remember to use a capital letter?

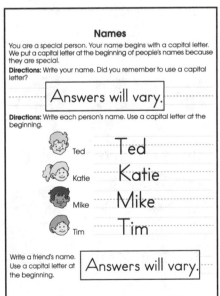

Answers will vary.

Directions: Write each person's name. Use a capital letter at the beginning.

Ted   Ted

Katie   Katie

Mike   Mike

Tim   Tim

Write a friend's name. Use a capital letter at the beginning.

Answers will vary.

Page 59

Names: Days of the Week

The days of the week begin with capital letters.

Directions: Write the days of the week in the spaces below. Put them in order. Be sure to start with capital letters.

Tuesday
Saturday
Monday
Friday
Thursday
Sunday
Wednesday

	Sunday
	Monday
	Tuesday
	Wednesday
	Thursday
	Friday
	Saturday

Page 60

Names: Months of the Year

The months of the year begin with capital letters.

Directions: Write the months of the year in order on the calendar below. Be sure to use capital letters.

| January | December | April | May | October | June |
| September | February | July | March | November | August |

January	July
February	August
March	September
April	October
May	November
June	December

Page 61

More Than One

Directions: An **s** at the end of a word often means there is more than one. Look at each picture. Circle the correct word. Write the word on the line.

two dog (dogs)
four flower (flowers)
one bikes (bike)

dogs   flowers   bike

three (toys) toy
a (lamb) lambs
two cat (cats)

toys   lamb   cats

Page 62

More Than One

Directions: Read the nouns under the pictures. Then write each noun under **One** or **More Than One**.

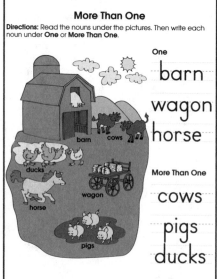

One
barn
wagon
horse

More Than One
cows
pigs
ducks

Page 64

More Than One

Directions: Choose the word which completes each sentence. Write each word on the line.

1. I have a ___dog___ .
   (dog) dogs

2. Four ___apples___ are on the tree.
   apple (apples)

3. I read two ___books___ today.
   book (books)

4. My ___bike___ is blue.
   (bike) bikes

5. We saw lots of ___monkeys___ at the zoo.
   monkey (monkeys)

6. I have five ___balloons___ .
   balloon (balloons)

Page 65

Riddles

Directions: Read the word. Trace and write it on the line. Then draw a line from the riddle to the animal it tells about.

long **long long**

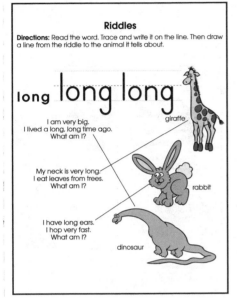

I am very big.
I lived a long, long time ago.
What am I?

My neck is very long.
I eat leaves from trees.
What am I?

giraffe

I have long ears.
I hop very fast.
What am I?

rabbit

dinosaur

Page 66

Riddles

Directions: Read the word and write it on the line. Then read each riddle and draw a line to the picture and word that tells about it.

house
house

kitten
kitten

flower
flower

pony
pony

I like to play.
I am little. I am soft.
What am I?
house

I am big.
You live in me.
What am I?
kitten

I am pretty.
I am green and yellow.
What am I?
flower

I can jump. I can run.
I am brown.
What am I?
pony

Page 67

Riddles

Directions: Write a word from the box to answer each riddle.

| ice cream | book | chair | sun |

There are many words in me.
I am fun to read.
What am I?

book

I am soft and yellow.
You can sit on me.
What am I?

chair

I am in the sky in the day.
I am hot. I am yellow.
What am I?

sun

I am cold. I am sweet.
You like to eat me.
What am I?

ice cream

Page 68

Picture Clues

Directions: Read the sentence. Circle the word that makes sense. Use the picture clues to help you. Then write the word.

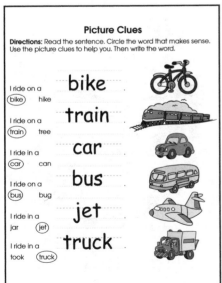

I ride on a
(bike) hike
bike

I ride on a
(train) tree
train

I ride in a
(car) can
car

I ride on a
(bus) bug
bus

I ride in a
jar (jet)
jet

I ride in a
took (truck)
truck

Page 69

Picture Clues

Directions: Read the sentence. Circle the word that makes sense. Use the picture clues to help you. Then write the word.

I see the
(bird) book
bird

I see the
(fish) fork
fish

I see the
(dogs) dig
dogs

I see the
(cats) coats
cats

I see the
(snake) snow
snake

I see the
(rat) rake
rat

Page 70

Comprehension

Directions: Look at the picture. Write the words from the box to finish the sentences.

| frog | log | bird | fish | ducks |

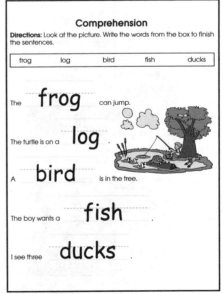

The **frog** can jump.

The turtle is on a **log**

A **bird** is in the tree.

The boy wants a **fish**

I see three **ducks**

Page 71

Comprehension

Directions: Read the poem. Write the correct words in the blanks.

A Poem
The hat was on a mat.
A cat sat on the hat.
Now the hat is flat.

The hat was on   **a mat**

Who sat on the hat?   **a cat**

Now the hat is   **flat**

Page 72

Following Directions: Colour the Path

Directions: Colour the path the girl should take to go home. Use the sentences to help you.

1. Go to the school and turn left.
2. At the end of the street, turn right.
3. Walk past the park and turn right.
4. After you pass the pool, turn right.

Page 73

Following Directions

Directions: Look at the pictures. Follow the directions in each box.

Draw a circle around the caterpillar. Draw a line under the stick.

Draw an **X** on the mother bird. Draw a triangle around the baby birds.

Draw a box around the rabbit.

Colour the flowers. Count the bees. There are __2__ bees.

Page 74

Classifying

Directions: Classifying is sorting things into groups. Draw a circle around the pictures that answer the question.

What Can Swim?

What Can Fly?

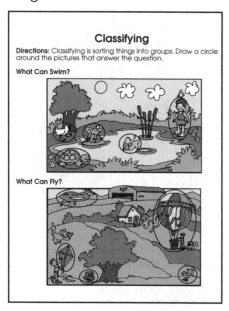

Page 75

Classifying: These Keep Me Warm

Directions: Colour the things that keep you warm.

socks
apple
lunch box
earmuffs
cookie
hat
coat
umbrella
gloves
book

Page 76

Classifying: Objects

Help Dan clean up the park.

Directions: Circle the litter. Underline the coins. Draw a box around the balls.

Page 77

Classifying: Things to Drink

Directions: Circle the pictures of things you can drink. Write the names of those things in the blanks.

milk   ice   soup and crackers

juice   soda   ice-cream bar

milk
juice   soda

Page 78

Vocabulary

Directions: Read the words. Trace and write them on the lines. Look at each picture. Write **hot** or **cold** on the lines to show if it is hot or cold.

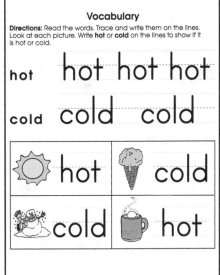

hot   hot hot hot

cold   cold cold

hot | cold
cold | hot

Page 79

Vocabulary

Directions: Read the words. Trace and write them on the lines. Look at each picture and write **day** or **night** on the lines to show if they happen during the day or night.

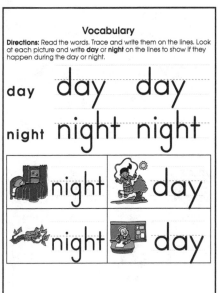

day   day day

night   night night

night | day
night | day

Page 80

Classifying: Night and Day

Directions: Write the words from the box under the pictures they describe.

stars   sun   moon   rays   dark   light   night   day

stars   sun
moon   rays
dark   light
night   day

Page 81

Classifying: Clowns and Balloons

Some words describe clowns. Some words describe balloons.

Directions: Read the words. Write the words that match in the correct columns.

| float | laughs | hat | string |
| air | feet | pop | nose |

clown   balloons

laughs   float
feet   air
hat   pop
nose   string

Page 82

Similarities: Objects

Directions: Circle the picture in each row that is most like the first picture.

Example:

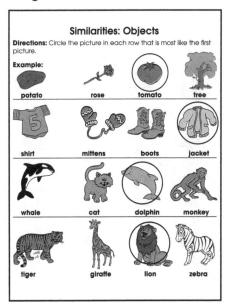

potato   rose   tomato   tree

shirt   mittens   boots   jacket

whale   cat   dolphin   monkey

tiger   giraffe   lion   zebra

Page 83

Similarities: Objects

Directions: Circle the picture in each row that is most like the first picture.

Example:

carrot — jacks — bread — pea

baseball — sneakers — basketball — bat

store — school — home — bakery

kitten — dog — fox — cat

Page 84

Classifying: Food Groups

Directions: Colour the meats and eggs blue. Colour the fruits and vegetables green. Colour the breads tan. Colour the dairy foods (milk and cheese) yellow.

fish — bread — apple — cheese

crackers — carrot — orange — eggs

steaks — pear — milk — yogurt

ice cream — chicken — potato — pretzel

Page 85

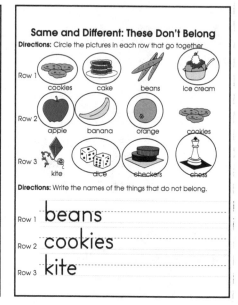

Same and Different: These Don't Belong

Directions: Circle the pictures in each row that go together.

Row 1: cookies — cake — beans — ice cream

Row 2: apple — banana — orange — cookies

Row 3: kite — dice — checkers — chess

Directions: Write the names of the things that do not belong.

Row 1: beans

Row 2: cookies

Row 3: kite

Page 86

Classifying: What Does Not Belong?

Directions: Draw an **X** on the picture that does not belong in each group.

fruit
apple — peach — corn — watermelon

wild animals
bear — kitten — gorilla — lion

pets
cat — fish — elephant — dog

flowers
grass — rose — daisy — tulip

Page 87

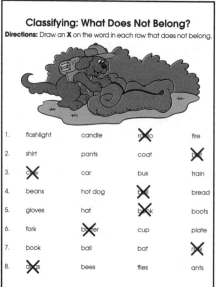

Classifying: What Does Not Belong?

Directions: Draw an **X** on the word in each row that does not belong.

1. flashlight — candle — radio — fire
2. shirt — pants — coat — X
3. X — car — bus — train
4. beans — hot dog — ball — bread
5. gloves — hat — book — boots
6. fork — butter — cup — plate
7. book — ball — bat — X
8. dogs — bees — flies — ants

Page 88

Classifying: Objects

Directions: Write each word in the correct row at the bottom of the page.

airplane — drum — radio — plate — car — pencil

spoon — crayon — chalk — fork — television — boat

Things we ride in:

airplane, car, boat

Things we eat with:

plate, spoon, fork

Things we draw with:

pencil, crayon, chalk

Things we listen to:

drum, radio, television

Complete Early Skills Grade 1

Answer Key

Page 89

Classifying: Names, Numbers, Animals, Colors

Directions: Write the words from the box next to the words they describe.

Joe	cat	blue	Tim
two	dog	red	ten
Sue	green	pig	six

Name Words

Joe   Tim   Sue

Number Words

two   ten   six

Animal Words

cat   dog   pig

Color Words

green   red   blue

Page 90

Classifying: Things That Belong Together

Directions: Circle the pictures in each row that belong together.

Row 1   knife   key   fork   spoon

Row 2   orange   apple   candy   banana

Row 3   beach ball   soccer ball   baseball   apple

Directions: Write the names of the pictures that do not belong.

Row 1   key

Row 2   candy

Row 3   apple

Page 91

Classifying: Why They Are Different

Directions: Look at your answers on page 90. Write why each object does not belong.

You don't eat with a key.
A candy is not a fruit.
An apple is not a ball.

Directions: For each object, draw a group of pictures that belong with it.

Drawings will vary.

candy bar

Drawings will vary.

lettuce

Page 92

Classifying: What Does Not Belong?

Directions: Circle the two things that do not belong in the picture. Write why they do not belong.

1. Flowers do not grow in snow.

2. Palm trees do not grow in snow.

Page 93

Sequencing: Fill the Glasses

Directions: Follow the instructions to fill each glass. Use crayons to draw your favourite drink in the ones that are full and half-full.

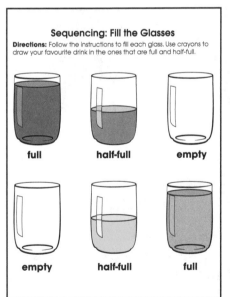

full   **half-full**   **empty**

empty   **half-full**   **full**

Page 94

Sequencing: Raking Leaves

Directions: Write a number in each box to show the order of the story.

Page 95

Sequencing: Make a Snowman!

Directions: Write the number of the sentence that goes with each picture in the box.

1. Roll a large snowball for the snowman's bottom.
2. Make another snowball and put it on top of the first.
3. Put the last snowball on top.
4. Dress the snowman.

Page 96

Sequencing: A Recipe

Directions: Look at the recipe below. Put each step in order. Write **1, 2, 3** or **4** in the box.

HOW TO MAKE BREAD BUDDIES

What kind of bread buddy did you make?

Answers will vary.

Page 97

Sequencing: How Flowers Grow

Directions: Read the story. Then write the steps to grow a flower.

First find a sunny spot. Then plant the seed. Water it. The flower will start to grow. Pull the weeds around it. Remember to keep giving the flower water. Enjoy your flower.

1. Find a sunny spot
2. Plant the seed
3. Water it
4. Pull the weeds
5. Enjoy your flower

Page 98

Comprehension: Apples

Directions: Read about apples. Then write the answers.

1. How many kinds of apples does the story tell about?

three

2. Name the kinds of apples.

red   green   yellow

3. What kind of apple do you like best?

Answers will vary.

Page 99

Comprehension: Crayons

Directions: Read about crayons. Then write your answers.

Crayons come in many colours. Some crayons are dark colours. Some crayons are light colours. All crayons have wax in them.

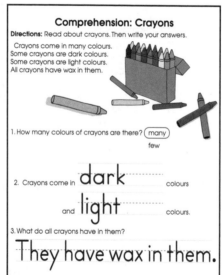

1. How many colours of crayons are there? (many) few

2. Crayons come in **dark** colours

and **light** colours.

3. What do all crayons have in them?

They have wax in them.

Page 100

Comprehension

Directions: Read the story. Write the words from the story that complete each sentence.

Jane and Bill like to play in the rain. They take off their shoes and socks. They splash in the puddles. It feels cold! It is fun to splash!

Jane and Bill like to **play in the rain**

They take off their **shoes and socks**

They splash in **the puddles**

Do you like to splash in puddles? (Yes) No

Page 101

Comprehension

Directions: Read the story. Write the words from the story that complete each sentence.

Ben and Sue have a bug.
It is red with black spots.
They call it Spot.
Spot likes to eat green leaves and grass.
The children keep Spot in a box.

Ben and Sue have a __bug__

It is __red__ with black spots.

The bug's name is __Spot__

The bug eats __green leaves and grass__

Page 102

Comprehension: Growing Flowers

Directions: Read about flowers. Then write the answers.

Some flowers grow in pots. Many flowers grow in flower beds. Others grow beside the road. Flowers begin from seeds. They grow into small buds. Then they open wide and bloom. Flowers are pretty!

Answers may include:

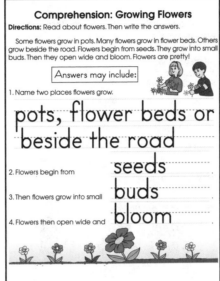

1. Name two places flowers grow.

__pots, flower beds or beside the road__

2. Flowers begin from __seeds__

3. Then flowers grow into small __buds__

4. Flowers then open wide and __bloom__

Page 103

Comprehension: Raking Leaves

Directions: Read about raking leaves. Then answer the questions.

I like to rake leaves. Do you? Leaves die each year. They get brown and dry. They fall from the trees. Then we rake them up.

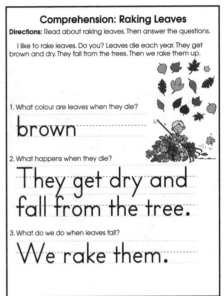

1. What colour are leaves when they die?

__brown__

2. What happens when they die?

__They get dry and fall from the tree.__

3. What do we do when leaves fall?

__We rake them.__

Page 104

Comprehension: Clocks

Directions: Read about clocks. Then answer the questions.

Ticking Clocks

Many clocks make two sounds. The sounds are tick and tock. Big clocks often make loud tick-tocks. Little clocks often make quiet tick-tocks. Sometimes people put little clocks in a box with a new puppy. The puppy likes the sound. The tick-tock makes the puppy feel safe.

1. What two sounds do many clocks make?

__tick__ and __tock__

2. What kind of tick-tocks do big clocks make?

__loud tick tocks__

3. What kind of clock makes a new puppy feel safe?

__a little clock__

Page 105

Comprehension: Soup

Directions: Read about soup. Then write the answers.

I Like Soup

Soup is good! It is good for you, too. We eat most kinds of soup hot. Some people eat cold soup in the summer. Carrots and beans are in some soups. Do you like crackers with soup?

1. Name two ways people eat soup.

__cold__   __hot__

2. Name two things that are in some soups.

__carrots__   __beans__

3. Name the kind of soup you like best.

Answers will vary.

Page 106

Comprehension: The Teddy Bear Song

Do you know the Teddy Bear Song? It is very old!

Directions: Read the Teddy Bear Song. Then answer the questions.

Teddy bear, teddy bear, turn around.
Teddy bear, teddy bear, touch the ground.
Teddy bear, teddy bear, climb upstairs.
Teddy bear, teddy bear, say your prayers.
Teddy bear, teddy bear, turn out the light.
Teddy bear, teddy bear, say, "Good night!"

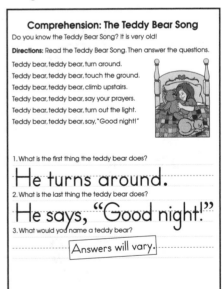

1. What is the first thing the teddy bear does?

__He turns around.__

2. What is the last thing the teddy bear does?

__He says, "Good night!"__

3. What would you name a teddy bear?

Answers will vary.

Page 107

Sequencing: Put Teddy Bear to Bed

Directions: Read the song about the teddy bear again. Write a number in each box to show the order of the story.

3 4

1 2

Page 108

Comprehension: A New Teddy Bear Song

Directions: Write words to make a new teddy bear song. Act out your new song with your teddy bear as you read it.

Answers will vary.

Teddy bear, teddy bear, turn

Teddy bear, teddy bear, touch the

Teddy bear, teddy bear, climb

Teddy bear, teddy bear, turn out

Teddy bear, teddy bear, say,

Page 109

Sequencing: Petting a Cat

Directions: Read the story. Then write the answers.

Do you like cats? I do. To pet a cat, move slowly. Hold out your hand. The cat will come to you. Then pet its head. Do not grab a cat! It will run away.

To pet a cat . . .

1. Move **slowly**

2. Hold out your **hand**

3. The cat will come to **you**

4. Pet the cat's **head**

5. Do not **grab** a cat!

Page 110

Comprehension: Cats

Directions: Read the story about cats again. Then write the answers.

1. What is a good title for the story?

Answers will vary.

2. The story tells you how to **pet a cat**

3. What part of your body should you pet a cat with?

your hand

4. Why should you move slowly to pet a cat?

Answers will vary.

5. Why do you think a cat will run away if you grab it?

Answers will vary.

Page 111

Comprehension: Cats

Directions: Look at the pictures and read about four cats. Then write the correct name beside each cat.

Fluffy, Blackie and Tiger are playing. Tom is sleeping. Blackie has spots. Tiger has stripes.

Fluffy

Tiger

Blackie

Tom

Page 112

Same and Different: Cats

Directions: Compare the picture of the cats on page 111 to this picture. Write a word from the box to tell what is different about each cat.

| purple ball | green bow | blue brush | red collar |

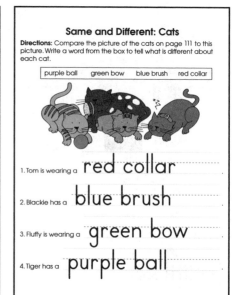

1. Tom is wearing a **red collar**

2. Blackie has a **blue brush**

3. Fluffy is wearing a **green bow**

4. Tiger has a **purple ball**

Page 113

Comprehension: Tigers

Directions: Read about tigers. Then write the answers.

Tigers sleep during the day. They hunt at night. Tigers eat meat. They hunt deer. They like to eat wild pigs. If they cannot find meat, tigers will eat fish.

1. When do tigers sleep?

during the day

2. Name two things tigers eat. *Answers may include:*

meat, deer, wild pigs or fish

3. When do tigers hunt? at night

Page 114

Following Directions: Tiger Puzzle

Directions: Read the story about tigers again. Then complete the puzzle.

```
¹F I ²S H
    L
  ³M E A T
    E
  ⁴P I G
```

Across:

1. When tigers cannot get meat, they eat _____ .
3. The food tigers like best is _____ .
4. Tigers like to eat this meat: wild _____ .

Down:

2. Tigers do this during the day.

Page 115

Following Directions: Draw a Tiger

Directions: Follow directions to complete the picture of the tiger.

1. Draw black stripes on the tiger's body and tail.
2. Colour the tiger's tongue red.
3. Draw claws on the feet.
4. Draw a black nose and two black eyes on the tiger's face.
5. Colour the rest of the tiger orange.
6. Draw tall, green grass for the tiger to sleep in.

Page 116

Comprehension: Write a Party Invitation

Directions: Read about the party. Then complete the invitation.

The party will be at Dog's house. The party will start at 1:00 P.M. It will last 2 hours. Write your birthday for the date of the party.

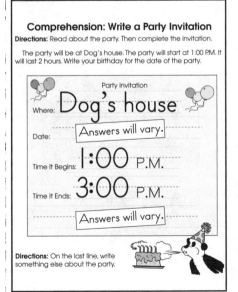

Party Invitation

Where: Dog's house

Date: Answers will vary.

Time It Begins: 1:00 P.M.

Time It Ends: 3:00 P.M.

Answers will vary.

Directions: On the last line, write something else about the party.

Page 117

Sequencing: Pig Gets Ready

Directions: Number the pictures of Pig getting ready for the party to show the order of the story.

What kind of party do you think Pig is going to?   Answers will vary.

Page 118

Comprehension: An Animal Party

Directions: Use the picture for clues. Write words from the box to answer the questions.

bear	cat
dog	elephant
giraffe	hippo
pig	tiger

1. Which animals have bow ties?

cat   tiger

2. Which animal has a hat?

bear

3. Which animal has a striped shirt?

pig

Page 119

Classifying: Party Items

Directions: Draw a ☐ around objects that are food for the party. Draw a △ around the party guests. Draw a ◯ around the objects used for fun at the party.

Page 120

Comprehension: Rhymes

Directions: Read about words that rhyme. Then circle the answers.

Words that rhyme have the same end sounds. "Wing" and "sing" rhyme. "Boy" and "toy" rhyme. "Dime" and "time" rhyme. Can you think of other words that rhyme?

1. Words that rhyme have the same (end sounds.)
   end letters.

2. "Time" rhymes with "tree."
   ("dime.")

Directions: Write one rhyme for each word.

wing | Answers will vary. | boy

dime | pink

Page 121

Rhyming Words

Many poems have rhyming words. The rhyming words are usually at the end of the line.

Directions: Complete the poem with words from the box.

My Glue

I spilled my **glue**

I felt **blue**

What could I **do** ?

Hey! I have a **clue** !

I'll make it **clean**

The cleanest you've **seen**

No one will **scream**

Wouldn't that be **mean** ?

| blue | clue | scream | seen |
| glue | do | clean | mean |

Page 122

Classifying: Rhymes

Directions: Circle the pictures in each row that rhyme.

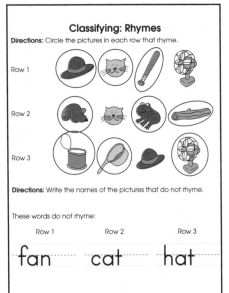

Row 1

Row 2

Row 3

Directions: Write the names of the pictures that do not rhyme.

These words do not rhyme:

Row 1 — Row 2 — Row 3

fan **cat** **hat**

Page 123

Predicting: Words and Pictures

Directions: Complete each story by choosing the correct picture. Draw a line from the story to the picture.

1. Shawnda got her books. She went to the bus stop. Shawnda got on the bus.

2. Marco planted a seed. He watered it. He pulled the weeds around it.

3. Abraham's dog was barking. Abraham got out the dog food. He put it in the dog bowl.

Page 124

Predicting: Story Ending

Directions: Read the story. Draw a picture in the last box to complete the story.

That's my ball. | I got it first.

Pictures will vary.

It's mine!

Page 125

Predicting: Story Ending

Directions: Read the story. Draw a picture in the last box to complete the story.

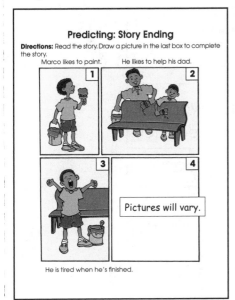

Marco likes to paint. **1** | He likes to help his dad. **2**

3 | **4** Pictures will vary.

He is tired when he's finished.

Page 126

Predicting: Story Ending

Directions: Read each story. Circle the sentence that tells how the story will end.

Ann was riding her bike. She saw a dog in the park. She stopped to pet it. Ann left to go home.

The dog went swimming.

(The dog followed Ann.)

The dog went home with a cat.

Antonio went to a baseball game. A baseball player hit a ball toward him. He reached out his hands.

The player caught the ball.

The ball bounced on a car.

(Antonio caught the ball.)

Page 127

Making Inferences: Baseball

Traci likes baseball. She likes to win. Traci's team does not win.

Directions: Circle the correct answers.

1. Traci likes
   football.   soccer.   (baseball.)

2. Traci likes to
   win.   lose.

3. Traci uses a bat.
   Yes   No

4. Traci is
   happy.   (sad.)

Page 128

Making Inferences: The Stars

Lynn looks at the stars. She sings a song about them. She makes a wish on them. The stars help Lynn sleep.

Directions: Circle the correct answers.

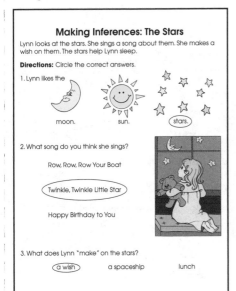

1. Lynn likes the
   moon.   sun.   (stars.)

2. What song do you think she sings?
   Row, Row, Row Your Boat
   (Twinkle, Twinkle Little Star)
   Happy Birthday to You

3. What does Lynn "make" on the stars?
   (a wish)   a spaceship   lunch

Page 129

Making Inferences: Feelings

Directions: Read each story. Choose a word from the box to show how each person feels.

happy	excited	sad	mad

1. Andy and Sam were best friends. Sam and his family moved far away. How does Sam feel?

   sad

2. Deana could not sleep. It was the night before her birthday party. How does Deana feel?

   excited

3. Jacob let his baby brother play with his teddy bear. His brother lost the bear. How does Jacob feel?

   mad

4. Kia picked flowers for her mom. Her mom smiled when she got them. How does Kia feel?

   happy

Page 130

Books

Directions: What do you know about books? Use the words in the box below to help fill in the lines.

title	book	author
illustrator	pages	left to right
fun	library	glossary

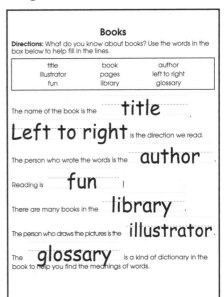

The name of the book is the **title**

Left to right is the direction we read.

The person who wrote the words is the **author**

Reading is **fun** !

There are many books in the **library**.

The person who draws the pictures is the **illustrator**.

The **glossary** is a kind of dictionary in the book to help you find the meanings of words.

Page 132

Nouns

A noun is a word that names a person, place or thing. When you read a sentence, the noun is what the sentence is about.

Directions: Complete each sentence with a noun.

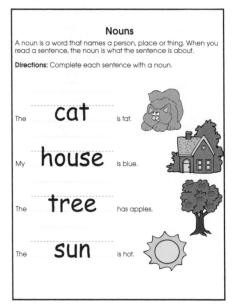

The **cat** is fat.

My **house** is blue.

The **tree** has apples.

The **sun** is hot.

Page 133

Nouns

Directions: Write these naming words in the correct box.

| store | zoo | child | baby | teacher | table |
| cat | park | gym | woman | sock | horse |

Person	**child** **woman** **baby** **teacher**
Place	**store** **park** **zoo** **gym**
Thing	**sock** **horse** **table** **cat**

Page 134

Things That Go Together

Some nouns name things that go together.

Directions: Draw a line to match the nouns on the left with the things they go with on the right.

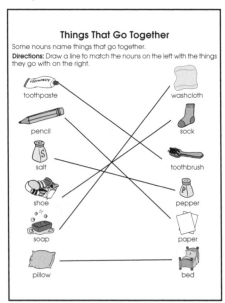

toothpaste — washcloth

pencil — sock

salt — toothbrush

shoe — pepper

soap — paper

pillow — bed

Page 135

Tracking: Things That Go Together

Directions: Draw a line to connect the objects that go together.

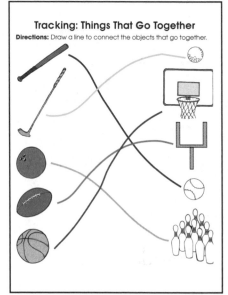

Page 136

Verbs

Verbs are words that tell what a person or a thing can do.

Example: The girl pats the dog.
The word **pats** is the verb. It shows action.

Directions: Draw a line between the verbs and the pictures that show the action.

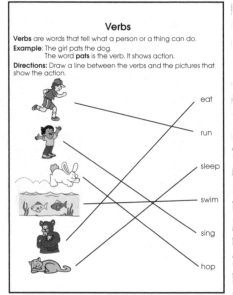

eat

run

sleep

swim

sing

hop

Page 137

Verbs

Directions: Look at the picture and read the words. Write an action word in each sentence below.

1. The two boys like to __talk__ together.
2. The children __kick__ the soccer ball.
3. Some children like to __swing__ on the swing.
4. The girl can __run__ very fast.
5. The teacher __rings__ the bell.

Page 138

Words That Describe

Describing words tell us more about a person, place or thing.
Directions: Read the words in the box. Choose the word that describes the picture. Write it next to the picture.

| happy | round | sick | cold | long |

long
happy
sick
round
cold

Page 139

Words That Describe

Directions: Read the words in the box. Choose the word that describes the picture. Write it next to the picture.

| wet | round | funny | soft | sad | tall |

soft · tall
funny · sad
round · wet

Page 140

Words That Describe

Directions: Circle the describing word in each sentence. Draw a line from the sentence to the picture.

1. The hungry dog is eating.
2. The tiny bird is flying.
3. Horses have long legs.
4. She is a fast runner.
5. The little boy was lost.

Page 141

Words That Describe: Colours and Numbers

Colours and numbers can describe nouns.
Directions: Underline the describing word in each sentence. Draw a picture to go with each sentence.

A <u>yellow</u> moon was in the sky.

Pictures will vary.

<u>Two</u> worms are on the road.

The tree had <u>red</u> apples.

The girl wore a <u>blue</u> dress.

Page 142

Sequencing: Comparative Adjectives

Directions: Look at each group of pictures. Write 1, 2 or 3 under the picture to show where it should be.

Example:

tallest 3 · tall 1 · taller 2
small 1 · smallest 3 · smaller 2
biggest 3 · big 1 · bigger 2
wider 2 · wide 1 · widest 3

325 Complete Early Skills Grade 1

Page 143

Sequencing: Comparative Adjectives

Directions: Look at the pictures in each row. Write 1, 2 or 3 under the picture to show where it should be.

shortest __3__   shorter __2__   short __1__

longest __3__   longer __2__   long __1__

happy __1__   happier __2__   happiest __3__

hotter __2__   hot __1__   hottest __3__

Page 144

Synonyms

Synonyms are words that mean almost the same thing. **Start** and **begin** are synonyms.

Directions: Find the synonyms that describe each picture. Write the words in the boxes below the picture.

small funny large sad silly little big unhappy	
small	large
little	big
sad	silly
unhappy	funny

Page 145

Similarities: Synonyms

Directions: Circle the word in each row that is most like the first word in the row.

Example:

grin		(smile)	frown	mad
bag		jar	(sack)	box
cat		fruit	(animal)	flower
apple		rot	cookie	(fruit)
around		(circle)	square	dot
brown		(tan)	black	red
bird		dog	cat	(duck)
bee		fish	(ant)	snake

Page 146

Synonyms

Directions: Read each sentence and look at the underlined word. Circle the word that means the same thing. Write the new words.

1. The boy was mad.   happy   (angry)   pup
2. The dog is brown.   (pup)   cat   rat
3. I like to scream.   soar   mad   (shout)
4. The bird can fly.   (soar)   jog   warm
5. The girl can run.   sleep   (jog)   shout
6. I am hot.   (warm)   cold   soar

angry	pup	shout
soar	jog	warm

Page 147

Similarities: Synonyms

Directions: Read the story. Write a word on the line that means almost the same as the word under the line.

Dan went to the _____ Answers will vary.
                    store

He wanted to buy _____
                    food

He walked very _____
                    quickly

The store had what he wanted.

He bought it using _____
                    dimes

Instead of walking home, Dan _____
                    jogged

Page 148

Antonyms

Antonyms are words that are opposites. **Hot** and **cold** are antonyms.
Directions: Draw a line between the antonyms.

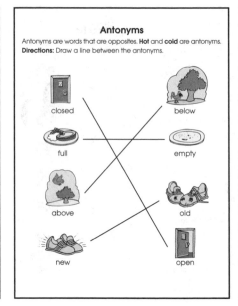

closed   below

full   empty

above   old

new   open

Page 149

Opposites

Directions: Draw lines to connect the words that are opposites.

up — down
over — under
dry — wet
clean — dirty

Page 150

Opposites

Opposites are things that are different in every way.

Directions: Draw a line between the opposites.

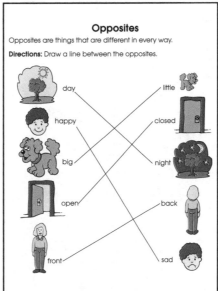

day — night
happy — sad
big — little
open — closed
front — back

Page 151

Opposites

Directions: Circle the picture in each row that is the opposite of the first picture.

up   down   over   across
cold   frozen   hot   warm
in   beside   out   over
cloud   rain   storm   sun

Page 152

Opposites

Directions: Read each clue. Write the answers in the puzzle.

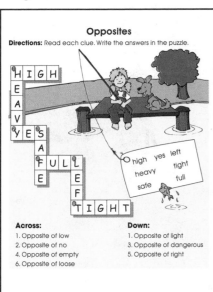

H I G H
HEAVY
YES
FULL
E
F
TIGHT

high   yes   left
heavy   tight
safe   full

Across:
1. Opposite of low
2. Opposite of no
4. Opposite of empty
6. Opposite of loose

Down:
1. Opposite of light
3. Opposite of dangerous
5. Opposite of right

Page 153

Homophones

Homophones are words that **sound** the same but are spelled differently and mean something different. **Blew** and **blue** are homophones.

Directions: Look at the word pairs. Choose the word that describes the picture. Write the word on the line next to the picture.

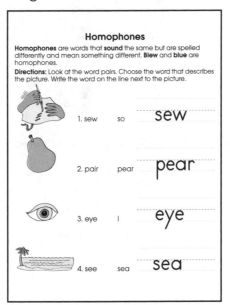

1. sew   so   **sew**

2. pair   pear   **pear**

3. eye   I   **eye**

4. see   sea   **sea**

Page 154

Homophones

Directions: Read each sentence. Underline the two words that sound the same but are spelled differently and mean something different.

1. Tom <u>ate</u> <u>eight</u> grapes.

2. Becky <u>read</u> Little <u>Red</u> Riding Hood.

3. I went <u>to</u> buy <u>two</u> dolls.

4. Five <u>blue</u> feathers <u>blew</u> in the wind.

5. <u>Would</u> you get <u>wood</u> for the fire?

Page 155

Sentences

Sentences begin with capital letters.

Directions: Read the sentences and write them below. Begin each sentence with a capital letter.

Example: the cat is fat.

The cat is fat.

my dog is big.

My dog is big.

the boy is sad.

The boy is sad.

bikes are fun!

Bikes are fun!

dad can bake.

Dad can bake.

Page 156

Word Order

If you change the order of the words in a sentence, you can change the meaning of the sentence.

Directions: Read the sentences. Draw a circle around the sentence that describes the picture.

Example:

(The fox jumped over the dogs.)
The dogs jumped over the fox.

1. (The cat watched the bird.)
The bird watched the cat.

2. (The girl looked at the boy.)
The boy looked at the girl.

3. The turtle ran past the rabbit.
(The rabbit ran past the turtle.)

Page 157

Word Order

Directions: Look at the picture. Put the words in order. Write the sentences on the lines below.

1. We made lemonade. some
2. good. It was
3. We the sold lemonade.
4. cost It five cents.
5. fun. We had

1. We made some lemonade.

2. It was good.

3. We sold the lemonade.

4. It cost five cents.

5. We had fun.

Page 158

Telling Sentences

Directions: Read the sentences and write them below. Begin each sentence with a capital letter. End each sentence with a period.

1. most children like pets
2. some children like dogs
3. some children like cats
4. some children like snakes
5. some children like all animals

1. Most children like pets.

2. Some children like dogs.

3. Some children like cats.

4. Some children like snakes.

5. Some children like all animals.

Page 159

Telling Sentences

Directions: Read the sentences and write them below. Begin each sentence with a capital letter. End each sentence with a period.

1. i like to go to the store with Mom
2. we go on Friday
3. i get to push the cart
4. i get to buy the cookies
5. i like to help Mom

1. I like to go to the store with Mom.

2. We go on Friday.

3. I get to push the cart.

4. I get to buy the cookies.

5. I like to help Mom.

Page 160

Asking Sentences

Directions: Write the first word of each asking sentence. Be sure to begin each question with a capital letter. End each question with a question mark.

1. Do _____ you like the zoo ?   do

2. How _____ much does it cost ?   how

3. Can _____ you feed the ducks ?   can

4. Will _____ you see the monkeys ?   will

5. What _____ time will you eat lunch ?   what

Page 161

Asking Sentences

Directions: Read the asking sentences. Write the sentences below. Begin each sentence with a capital letter. End each sentence with a question mark.

1. what game will we play
2. do you like to read
3. how old are you
4. who is your best friend
5. can you tie your shoes

1. What game will we play?
2. Do you like to read?
3. How old are you?
4. Who is your best friend?
5. Can you tie your shoes?

Page 162

Periods and Question Marks

Directions: Put a period or a question mark at the end of each sentence below.

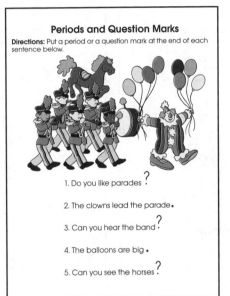

1. Do you like parades?
2. The clowns lead the parade.
3. Can you hear the band?
4. The balloons are big.
5. Can you see the horses?

Page 163

Is and Are

We use **is** in sentences about one person or one thing. We use **are** in sentences about more than one person or thing.

Example: The dog **is** barking.
The dogs **are** barking.

Directions: Write **is** or **are** in the sentences below.

1. Jim __is__ playing baseball.
2. Fred and Sam __are__ good friends.
3. Cupcakes __are__ my favourite treat.
4. Lisa __is__ a good soccer player.

Page 164

Is and Are

Directions: Write **is** or **are** in the sentences below.
Example: Lisa __is__ sleeping.

1. Cats and dogs __are__ good pets.
2. Bill __is__ my best friend.
3. Apples __are__ good to eat.
4. We __are__ going to the zoo.
5. Pedro __is__ coming to my house.
6. When __are__ you all going to the zoo?

Page 166

Colour Names

Directions: Trace the letters to write the name of each colour. Then write the name again by yourself.

Example:

orange	orange
blue	blue
green	green
yellow	yellow
red	red
brown	brown

Page 167

Colour Names: Sentences

Directions: Use the colour words to complete these sentences. Then put a period at the end.

Example: My new [mittens] are **orange**.

green tree	blue bike	yellow chick	red ball

1. The baby [chick] is **yellow** .
2. This [tree] is **green** .
3. My [ball] is big and **red** .
4. My sister's [bike] is **blue** .

Page 168

Animal Names

Directions: Fill in the missing letters for each word.

Example:

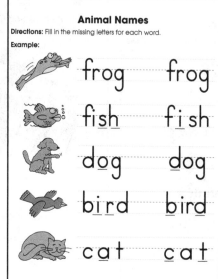

frog frog
fish fish
dog dog
bird bird
cat cat

Page 169

Animal Names: Sentences

A **sentence** tells about something.

Directions: These sentences tell about animals. Write the word that completes each sentence.

Example:

My **frog** jumps high.

1. I take my **dog** for a walk.
2. My **fish** lives in water.
3. My **bird** can sing.
4. My **cat** has a long tail.

Page 170

Things That Go

Directions: Trace the letters to write the name of each thing. Write each name again by yourself. Then colour the pictures.

Example:

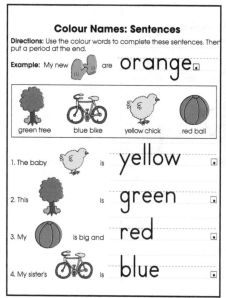

car car
truck truck
train train
bike bike
plane plane

Page 171

Things That Go: Sentences

Directions: These sentences tell about things that go. Write the word that completes each sentence.

Example:

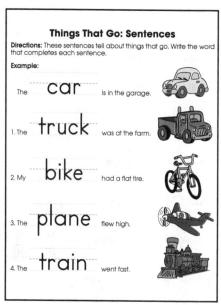

The **car** is in the garage.

1. The **truck** was at the farm.
2. My **bike** had a flat tire.
3. The **plane** flew high.
4. The **train** went fast.

Page 172

Clothing Words

Directions: Trace the letters to write the name of each clothing word. Then write each name again by yourself.

Example:

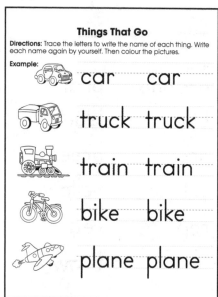

shirt shirt
pants pants
jacket jacket
socks socks
shoes shoes
dress dress
hat hat

Page 173

Clothing Words: Sentences

Directions: Some of these sentences tell a whole idea. Others have something missing. If something is missing, draw a line to the word that completes the sentence. Put a period at the end of each sentence.

Example:

She is wearing a polka-dot

holes.

1. The baseball player wore a

2. His pants were torn.

dress.

3. The socks had

4. The jacket had blue buttons.

hat.

5. The shoes were brown.

Page 174

Food Names

Directions: Trace the letters to write the name of each food word. Write each name again by yourself. Then colour the pictures.

Example:

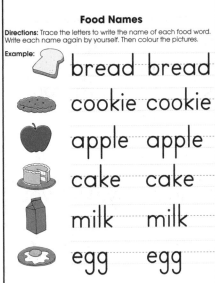

bread bread

cookie cookie

apple apple

cake cake

milk milk

egg egg

Page 175

Food Names: Asking Sentences

An **asking sentence** asks a question. Asking sentences end with a question mark.

Directions: Write each sentence on the line. Begin each sentence with a capital letter. Put a period at the end of the telling sentences and a question mark at the end of the asking sentences.

Example: do you like cake

Do you like cake?

1. the cow has spots

The cow has spots.

2. is that cookie good

Is that cookie good?

3. she ate the apple

She ate the apple.

Page 176

Number Words

Directions: Trace the letters to write the name of each number. Write the numbers again by yourself. Then colour the number pictures.

Example:
Colors will vary.

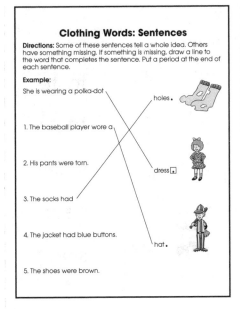

one one

two two

three three

four four

five five

six six

seven seven

eight eight

nine nine

ten ten

Page 177

Number Words: Asking Sentences

Directions: Use a number word to answer each question.

| one | five | seven | three | eight |

1. How many trees are there?

three

2. How many flowers are there?

seven

3. How many presents are there?

five

4. How many clocks are there?

one

5. How many forks are there?

eight

Page 178

Action Words

Action words tell things we can do.

Directions: Trace the letters to write each action word. Then write the action word again by yourself.

Example:

sleep sleep

run run

make make

ride ride

play play

stop stop

Page 179

Action Words: More Than One

To show more than one of something, add **s** to the end of the word.

Example: one cat   two cats

Directions: In each sentence, add **s** to show more than one. Then write the action word that completes each sentence.

sit	jump	stop	ride

Example:

The frog   s   **sleep**   in the sun.

1. The boy   s   **sit**   on the fence.

2. The car   s   **stop**   at the sign.

3. The girl   s   **swim**   in the water.

4. The dog   s   **sit**   in the wagon.

Page 180

Action Words: Asking Sentences

Directions: Write an asking sentence about each picture. Begin each sentence with **can**. Add an action word. Begin each asking sentence with a capital letter and end it with a question mark.

Example:
I with you can

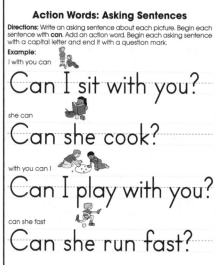

Can I sit with you?

she can

Can she cook?

with you can I

Can I play with you?

can she fast

Can she run fast?

Page 181

Sense Words

Directions: Circle the word that is spelled correctly. Then write the correct spelling in the blank.

Example:

tast / (taste) / tste   taste

(touch) / tuch / touh   touch

smel / smll / (smell)   smell

her / (hear) / har   hear

(see) / se / sea   see

Page 182

Sense Words: Sentences

Directions: Read each sentence and write the correct words in the blanks.

Example:

taste / mouth   I can **taste** things with my **mouth**.

touch / hands   1. I can **touch** things with my **hands**.

nose / smell   2. I can **smell** things with my **nose**.

hear / ears   3. I can **hear** with my **ears**.

see / eyes   4. I can **see** things with my **eyes**.

Page 183

Weather Words: Beginning Sounds

Directions: Say the sound of the letter at the beginning of each row. Find the pictures in each row that begin with the same letter. Write the letter under the pictures.

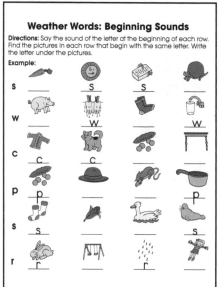

Example:

s   ___   S   S   ___

w   ___   W   ___   W

c   C   C   ___   ___

p   p   ___   ___   p

s   s   ___   ___   s

r   r   ___   ___   r

Page 184

Weather Words: Sentences

Directions: Write the weather word that completes each sentence. Put a period at the end of the telling sentences and a question mark at the end of the asking sentences.

Example:
Do flowers grow in the **sun** ?

rain	water	wet	hot

1. The sun makes me **hot** .

2. When it rains, the grass gets **wet** .

3. Do you think it will **rain** on our picnic ?

4. Should you drink the **water** from the rain ?

Page 185

My World

Directions: Fill in the missing letters for each word.

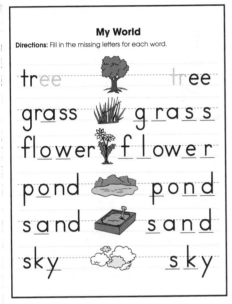

tree   tree

grass   grass

flower   flower

pond   pond

sand   sand

sky   sky

Page 186

My World

Directions: The letters in the words below are mixed up. Unscramble the letters and write each word correctly.

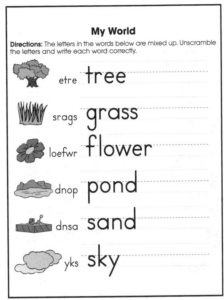

etre   tree

srags   grass

loefwr   flower

dnop   pond

dnsa   sand

yks   sky

Page 187

My World: Sentences

Directions: Write the word that completes each sentence. Put a period at the end of the telling sentences and a question mark at the end of the asking sentences.

Example: Does the sun shine on the **flowers**?

tree	grass	pond	sand	sky

1. The **sky** was full of dark clouds.

2. Can you climb the **tree**?

3. Did you see the duck in the **pond**?

4. Is the child playing in the **sand**?

5. The **grass** in the yard was tall.

Page 188

The Parts of My Body: Sentences

Directions: Write the word that completes each sentence. Put a period at the end of the telling sentences and a question mark at the end of the asking sentences.

Example: I wear my hat on my **head**.

arms	legs	feet	hands

1. How strong are your **arms**?

2. You wear shoes on your **feet**.

3. If you're happy and you know it, clap your **hands**.

4. My pants covered my **legs**.

Page 189

The Parts of My Body: Sentences

Directions: Read the sentence parts below. Draw a line from the first part of the sentence to the second part that completes it.

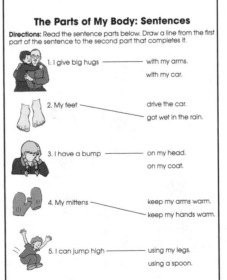

1. I give big hugs —— with my arms.
   with my car.

2. My feet —— drive the car.
   got wet in the rain.

3. I have a bump —— on my head.
   on my coat.

4. My mittens —— keep my arms warm.
   keep my hands warm.

5. I can jump high —— using my legs.
   using a spoon.

Page 190

The Parts of My Body: Sentences

Directions: Read the two sentences on each line and draw a line between them. Then write each sentence again on the lines below. Begin each sentence with a capital letter, and end each one with a period or a question mark.

Example: wash your hands|they are dirty

Wash your hands.

They are dirty.

1. you have big arms|are you very strong

You have big arms.

Are you very strong?

2. I have two feet|I can run fast

I have two feet.

I can run fast.

Page 192

Number Recognition

Directions: Write the numbers 1-10. Colour the bear.

1 2 3 4 5 6 7 8 9 10

Page 193

Number Recognition

Directions: Count the number of objects in each group. Draw a line to the correct number.

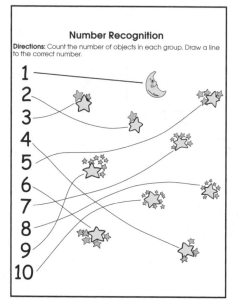

Page 194

Counting

Directions: How many are there of each shape? Write the answers in the boxes. The first one is done for you.

Page 195

Counting

Directions: How many are there of each picture? Write the answers in the boxes. The first one is done for you.

Page 196

Number Word Find

Directions: Find the number words 0 through 12 hidden in the box.

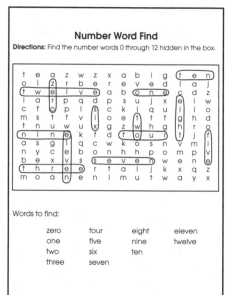

Words to find:

zero	four	eight	eleven
one	five	nine	twelve
two	six	ten	
three	seven		

Page 197

Number Words

Directions: Number the buildings from one to six.

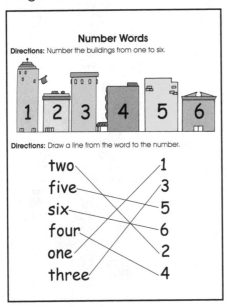

1 2 3 4 5 6

Directions: Draw a line from the word to the number.

two	1
five	3
six	5
four	6
one	2
three	4

Page 198

Number Words

Directions: Number the buildings from five to ten.

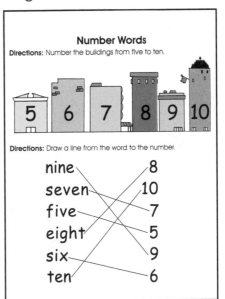

5 6 7 8 9 10

Directions: Draw a line from the word to the number.

nine	8
seven	10
five	7
eight	5
six	9
ten	6

Page 199

Number Recognition Review

Directions: Match the correct number of objects with the number. Then match the number with the word.

1	four
2	ten
3	two
4	six
5	one
6	nine
7	three
8	eight
9	five
10	seven

Page 200

Sequencing Numbers

Sequencing is putting numbers in the correct order.

1, 2, 3, 4, 5, 6, 7, 8, 9, 10

Directions: Write the missing numbers.

Example: 4, **5**, 6

3, **4**, 5   7, **8**, 9   8, **9**, 10

6, **7**, 8   **2**, 3, 4   **4**, 5, 6

5, 6, **7**   **5**, 6, 7   **2**, 3, 4

3, 4, 5   **6**, 7, 8   5, **6**, 7

2, 3, **4**   1, 2, **3**   7, 8, **9**

2, **3**, 4   **1**, 2, 3   4, **5**, 6

6, 7, **8**   3, 4, **5**   1, **2**, 3

7, 8, **9**   **2**, 3, 4   **8**, 9, 10

Page 201

Number Match

Directions: Cut out the pictures and number words below. Mix them up and match them again.

one	🌼	two	eight
🛒	🐛	five	🐝🐝🐝🐝
🐶🐶	three	🕐🕐🕐	nine
four	🥁🥁🥁	seven	🚂🚂🚂🚂🚂
🌐🌐🌐🌐🌐🌐	six	🐤🐤🐤🐤🐤🐤🐤	ten

Page 203

Number Crossword Puzzle

Directions: Write the correct number word in the boxes provided.

Across
2. 4
3. 8
5. 2
7. 7
9. 10

Down
1. 0
2. 5
4. 3
6. 1
7. 6
8. 9

one	two	three	four	five
•	••	•••	••••	•••••
six	seven	eight	nine	ten	zero
••• •••	•••• ••	•••• ••••	••••• ••••	••••• •••••	

Page 204

Ordinal Numbers

Ordinal numbers are used to indicate order in a series, such as **first**, **second** or **third**.

Directions: Draw a line to the picture that corresponds to the ordinal number in the left column.

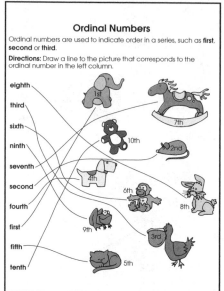

eighth
third
sixth
ninth
seventh
second
fourth
first
fifth
tenth

Page 205

Ordinal Numbers

Directions: Draw an **X** on the first vegetable, draw a circle around the second vegetable, and draw a square around the third vegetable.

Directions: Write the ordinal number below the picture.

1st 2nd 3rd 4th 5th 6th 7th 8th 9th 10th

✂ **Cut** the children apart. Mix them up. Then put them back in the correct order.

first | second | third | fourth | fifth | sixth | seventh | eighth | ninth | tenth

Page 207

Sequencing: At the Movies

Directions: The children are watching a movie. Read the sentences. Cut out the pictures below. Glue them where they belong in the picture.

1. The first child is eating popcorn.
2. The third child is eating candy.
3. The fourth child has a cup of fruit punch.
4. The second child is eating a big pretzel.

Page 209

Sequencing: Standing in Line

Directions: These children are waiting to see a movie. Look at them and follow the instructions.

1. Colour the person who is first in line yellow.
2. Colour the person who is last in line brown.
3. Colour the person who is second in line pink.
4. Circle the person who is at the end of the line.

Page 210

Addition 1, 2

Addition means "putting together" or adding two or more numbers to find the sum. "+" is a plus sign. It means to add the 2 numbers. "=" is an equals sign. It tells how much they are together.

Directions: Count the cats and tell how many.

Page 211

Addition

Directions: Count the shapes and write the numbers below to tell how many in all.

Page 212

Addition

Directions: Draw the correct number of dots next to the numbers in each problem. Add up the number of dots to find your answer.

Example:

Page 213

Addition 3, 4, 5, 6

Directions: Practise writing the numbers and then add. Draw dots to help, if needed.

3 3 3 3   2   1
4 4 4 4   +4   +4
5 5 5 5   ‾6‾ ‾5‾
6 6 6 6   3   1
           +2   +2
           ‾5‾ ‾3‾

Page 214

Addition 4, 5, 6, 7

Directions: Practise writing the numbers and then add. Draw dots to help, if needed.

4 4 4 4   2   3
5 5 5 5   +5   +1
6 6 6 6   ‾7‾ ‾4‾
7 7 7 7   4   2
           +1   +4
           ‾5‾ ‾6‾

Page 215

Addition 6, 7, 8

Directions: Practise writing the numbers and then add. Draw dots to help, if needed.

6 6 6 6   3   5
7 7 7 7   +4   +1
8 8 8 8   7   6

2   4
+6   +4
8   8

Page 216

Addition 7, 8, 9

Directions: Prastice writing the numbers and then add. Draw dots to help, if needed.

7 7 7 7   8   3
8 8 8 8   +1   +5
9 9 9 9   9   8

2   6
+7   +1
9   7

Page 217

Addition Table

Directions: Add across and down with a friend. Fill in the spaces.

+	0	1	2	3	4	5
0	0	1	2	3	4	5
1	1	2	3	4	5	6
2	2	3	4	5	6	7
3	3	4	5	6	7	8
4	4	5	6	7	8	9
5	5	6	7	8	9	10

Do you notice any number patterns in the Addition Table?

Page 218

Subtraction 1, 2, 3

Subtraction means "taking away" or subtracting one number from another. "–" is a minus sign. It means to subtract the second number from the first.
Directions: Practise writing the numbers and then subtract. Draw dots and cross them out, if needed.

1 1 1 1   3   4
2 2 2 2   -1   -3
3 3 3 3   2   1

2   3
-1   -2
1   1

Page 219

Subtraction 3, 4, 5, 6

Directions: Practise writing the numbers and then subtract. Draw dots and cross them out, if needed.

3 3 3 3   5   6
4 4 4 4   -2   -1
5 5 5 5   3   5
6 6 6 6

6   5
-3   -1
3   4

Page 220

Subtraction

Directions: Draw the correct number of dots next to the numbers in each problem. Cross out the ones subtracted to find your answer.

Example:

5
-2
3

2 - 1 = 1

4 - 2 = 2	8 -6 2
6 -1 5	3 - 1 = 2
9 - 6 = 3	4 -3 1

Page 221

Page 222

Page 223

Page 224

Page 225

Page 226

Page 227

Picture Problems: Subtraction

Directions: Solve the number problem under each picture.

6 - 2 = __4__

9 - 5 = __4__

7 - 2 = __5__

4 - 1 = __3__

8 - 1 = __7__

4 - 0 = __4__

Page 228

Picture Problems: Addition and Subtraction

Directions: Solve the number problem under each picture.

7 - 4 = __3__

1 + 4 = __5__

3 + 5 = __8__

8 - 1 = __7__

9 + 5 = __14__

6 - 3 = __3__

Page 229

Picture Problems: Addition and Subtraction

Directions: Solve the number problem under each picture. Write + or – to show if you should add or subtract.

How many in all?
4 + 5 = __9__

How many s in all?
7 + 5 = __12__

How many s are left?
12 - 3 = __9__

How many s are left?
15 - 8 = __7__

How many s in all?
5 + 8 = __13__

How many s are left?
11 - 4 = __7__

Page 230

Picture Problems: Addition and Subtraction

Directions: Solve the number problem under each picture. Write + or – to show if you should add or subtract.

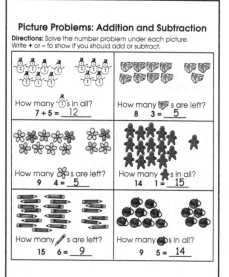

How many s in all?
7 + 5 = __12__

How many s are left?
8 – 3 = __5__

How many s are left?
9 – 4 = __5__

How many s in all?
14 – 1 = __15__

How many s are left?
15 – 6 = __9__

How many s in all?
9 – 5 = __14__

Page 231

Review: Addition and Subtraction

Directions: Solve the number problem under each picture. Write + or – to show if you should add or subtract.

How many s are left?
12 - 4 = __8__

How many s in all?
6 + 8 = __14__

How many s are left?
4 – 4 = __0__

How many s are left?
11 – 7 = __4__

How many s in all?
9 + 3 = __12__

How many s in all?
10 + 0 = __10__

Page 232

Addition 1-5

Directions: Count the tools in each tool box. Write your answers in the blanks. Circle the problem that matches your answer.

__4__   (2 +2)   2 +1

__6__   5 +0   (4 +2)

__8__   (6 +2)   4 +3

__5__   3 +1   (2 +3)

Page 233

Addition 1-5

Directions: Look at the red numbers and draw that many more flowers in the pot. Count them to get your total.

Example: 3 + 2 = __5__

1 + 4 = __5__

$$\begin{array}{r} 1 \\ +1 \\ \hline 2 \end{array}$$

$$\begin{array}{r} 2 \\ +2 \\ \hline 4 \end{array}$$

3 + 1 = __4__

Page 234

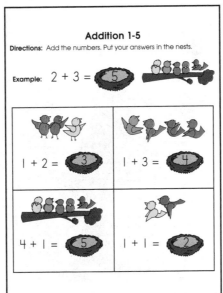

Addition 1-5

Directions: Add the numbers. Put your answers in the nests.

Example: 2 + 3 = __5__

1 + 2 = __3__

1 + 3 = __4__

4 + 1 = __5__

1 + 1 = __2__

Page 235

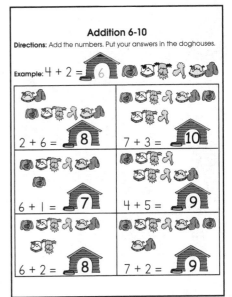

Addition 6-10

Directions: Add the numbers. Put your answers in the doghouses.

Example: 4 + 2 = __6__

2 + 6 = __8__

7 + 3 = __10__

6 + 1 = __7__

4 + 5 = __9__

6 + 2 = __8__

7 + 2 = __9__

Page 236

Subtraction 1-5

Directions: Subtract the red numbers by crossing out that many flowers in the pot. Count the ones not crossed out to get the total.

Example: 2 - 1 = __1__

5 - 2 = __3__

$$\begin{array}{r} 4 \\ -2 \\ \hline 2 \end{array}$$

$$\begin{array}{r} 3 \\ -1 \\ \hline 2 \end{array}$$

4 - 3 = __1__

Page 237

Subtraction 1-5

Directions: Count the fruit in each bowl. Write your answers on the blanks. Circle the problem that matches your answer.

$$\begin{array}{cc} 4 & \\ \underline{5} & 4 \\ -1 & -2 \end{array}$$

$$\begin{array}{cc} 3 & \\ \underline{3} & 4 \\ -0 & -2 \end{array}$$

$$\begin{array}{cc} 4 & \\ \underline{5} & 4 \\ -1 & -3 \end{array}$$

$$\begin{array}{cc} 5 & \\ 3 & 5 \\ -2 & -0 \end{array}$$

Page 238

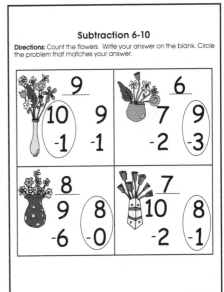

Subtraction 6-10

Directions: Count the flowers. Write your answer on the blank. Circle the problem that matches your answer.

$$\begin{array}{cc} 9 & \\ \underline{10} & 9 \\ -1 & -1 \end{array}$$

$$\begin{array}{cc} 6 & \\ 9 & 9 \\ -2 & -3 \end{array}$$

$$\begin{array}{cc} 8 & \\ 9 & 8 \\ -6 & -0 \end{array}$$

$$\begin{array}{cc} 7 & \\ 10 & 8 \\ -2 & -1 \end{array}$$

Page 239

Addition and Subtraction

Directions: Solve the problems. Remember, addition means "putting together" or adding two or more numbers to find the sum. Subtraction means "taking away" or subtracting one number from another.

1 + 3 = **4**   4 - 3 = **1**   4 + 5 = **9**

6 + 1 = **7**   7 - 2 = **5**   8 - 4 = **4**

9 - 1 = **8**   10 - 3 = **7**

5 - 2 = **3**   6 + 3 = **9**

8 + 2 = **10**   5 + 5 = **10**

Page 240

Addition and Subtraction

Remember, addition means "putting together" or adding two or more numbers to find the sum. Subtraction means "take away" or subtracting one number from another.

Directions: Solve the problems. From your answers, use the code to colour the quilt.

Color:
6 = blue
7 = yellow
8 = green
9 = red
10 = orange

Page 241

Place Value: Tens and Ones

The place value of a digit, or numeral, is shown by where it is in the number. For example, in the number **23**, **2** has the place value of **tens**, and **3** is ones.

Directions: Count the groups of ten crayons and write the number by the word **tens**. Count the other crayons and write the number by the word **ones**.

Example:

= **1** ten + **1** one

= **2** tens + **3** ones

= **4** tens + **8** ones

= **7** tens + **2** ones

6 tens + 3 ones = **63**   5 tens + 1 one = **51**

3 tens + 8 ones = **38**   9 tens + 7 ones = **97**

4 tens + 5 ones = **45**   2 tens + 8 ones = **28**

Page 242

Place Value: Tens and Ones

Directions: Count the groups of ten blocks and write the number by the word tens. Count the other blocks and write the number by the word ones.

Example:

+ = **1** ten + **2** ones

+ = **3** tens + **3** ones

+ = **5** tens + **6** ones

+ = **2** tens + **8** ones

+ = **7** tens + **2** ones

Page 243

Place Value: Tens and Ones

Directions: Write the answers in the correct spaces.

		tens	ones		
3 tens, 2 ones		3	2	=	32
3 tens, 7 ones		3	7	=	37
9 tens, 1 one		9	1	=	91
5 tens, 6 ones		5	6	=	56
6 tens, 5 ones		6	5	=	65
6 tens, 8 ones		6	8	=	68
2 tens, 8 ones		2	8	=	28
4 tens, 9 ones		4	9	=	49
1 ten, 4 ones		1	4	=	14
8 tens, 2 ones		8	2	=	82
4 tens, 2 ones		4	2	=	42

28 = **2** tens, **8** ones
64 = **6** tens, **4** ones
56 = **5** tens, **6** ones
72 = **7** tens, **2** ones
38 = **3** tens, **8** ones
17 = **1** ten, **7** ones
63 = **6** tens, **3** ones
12 = **1** ten, **2** ones

Page 244

Review: Place Value

The place value of each digit, or numeral, is shown by where it is in the number. For example, in the number **123**, **1** has the place value of **hundreds**, **2** is **tens** and **3** is **ones**.

Directions: Count the groups of crayons and add.

Example:

	Hundreds	Tens	Ones

= **1** **1** **3**

1 Hundred + 1 Ten + 3 Ones

+ + = **1** **2** **4**

+ + = **1** **3** **6**

GRADE 1

Page 245

Counting by Fives
Directions: Count by fives to draw the path to the playground.

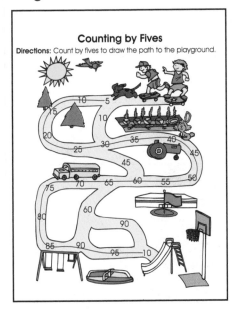

Page 246

Counting by Fives
Directions: Use tally marks to count by fives. Write the number next to the tallies.
Example: A tally mark stands for one = I. Five tally marks look like this = 卌

卌 __5__	卌 卌 卌 卌 卌 __35__
卌 卌 __10__	卌 卌 卌 卌 __40__ 卌 卌
卌 卌 卌 __15__	卌 卌 卌 卌 卌 卌 __45__
卌 卌 卌 卌 __20__	卌 卌 卌
卌 卌 卌 卌 卌 __25__	卌 卌 卌 卌 卌 卌 __50__ 卌
卌 卌 卌 卌 卌 卌 __30__	

Page 247

Counting by Tens
Directions: Count in order by tens to draw the path the boy takes to the store.

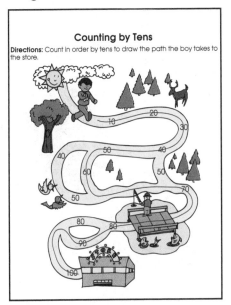

Page 248

Counting by Tens
Directions: Use the groups of 10's to count to 100.

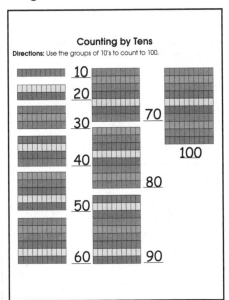

__10__
__20__
__30__
__40__
__50__
__60__
__70__
__80__
__90__
__100__

Page 249

Addition: 10-15
Directions: Circle groups of ten crayons. Add the remaining ones to make the correct number.

	tens	ones
+ =	3	9
+ =	5	7
+ =	4	6
+ =	6	7
+ =	7	8
+ =	9	6

6 + 6 = __12__   8 + 4 = __12__   9 + 5 = __14__

Page 250

Subtraction: 10-15
Directions: Count the crayons in each group. Put an X through the number of crayons being subtracted. How many are left?

	- 5	=	10
	- 4	=	☐
	- 7	=	☐
	- 6	=	☐
	- 5	=	☐
	- 8	=	☐

13 - 8 = ☐   11 - 5 = ☐   12 - 9 = ☐
14 - 7 = ☐   10 - 7 = ☐   13 - 3 = __10__
15 - 9 = ☐   11 - 8 = ☐   12 - 10 = ☐

Page 251

Shapes: Square

A square is a figure with four corners and four sides of the same length. This is a square ☐.

Directions: Find the squares and circle them.

Directions: Trace the word. Write the word.

square   square

Page 252

Shapes: Circle

A circle is a figure that is round. This is a circle ◯.

Directions: Find the circles and put a square around them.

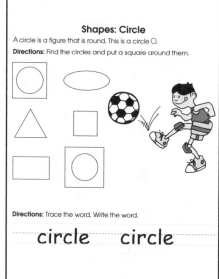

Directions: Trace the word. Write the word.

circle   circle

Page 253

Shapes: Square and Circle

Directions: Practice drawing squares. Trace the samples and make four of your own.

Directions: Practice drawing circles. Trace the samples and make four of your own.

Page 254

Shapes: Triangle

A triangle is a figure with three corners and three sides. This is a triangle △.

Directions: Find the triangles and put a circle around them.

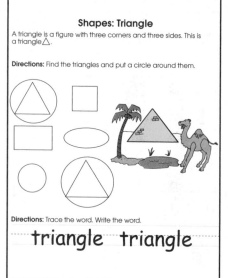

Directions: Trace the word. Write the word.

triangle   triangle

Page 255

Shapes: Rectangle

A rectangle is a figure with four corners and four sides. Sides opposite each other are the same length. This is a rectangle ☐.

Directions: Find the rectangles and put a circle around them.

Directions: Trace the word. Write the word.

rectangle rectangle

Page 256

Shapes: Triangle and Rectangle

Directions: Practice drawing triangles. Trace the samples and make four of your own.

Directions: Practice drawing rectangles. Trace the samples and make four of your own.

Page 257

Patterns: Rectangles

Directions: In each picture, there is more than one rectangle. Trace each rectangle with a different colour crayon. Under each picture, write how many rectangles you found.

_3_ rectangles

_3_ rectangles

Page 258

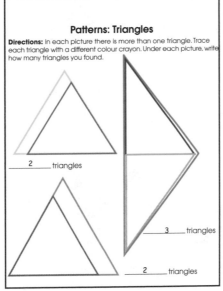

Patterns: Triangles

Directions: In each picture there is more than one triangle. Trace each triangle with a different colour crayon. Under each picture, write how many triangles you found.

_2_ triangles

_3_ triangles

_2_ triangles

Page 259

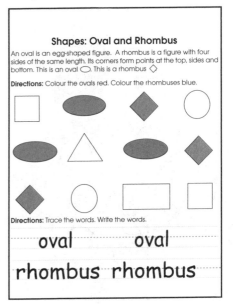

Shapes: Oval and Rhombus

An oval is an egg-shaped figure. A rhombus is a figure with four sides of the same length. Its corners form points at the top, sides and bottom. This is an oval ◯. This is a rhombus ◇

Directions: Colour the ovals red. Colour the rhombuses blue.

Directions: Trace the words. Write the words.

oval   oval

rhombus rhombus

Page 260

Shapes: Oval and Rhombus

Directions: Practice drawing ovals. Trace the samples and make four of your own.

Directions: Practice drawing rhombuses. Trace the samples and make four of your own.

Page 261

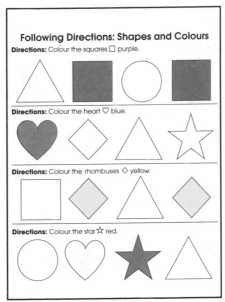

Following Directions: Shapes and Colours

Directions: Colour the squares ☐ purple.

Directions: Colour the heart ♡ blue.

Directions: Colour the rhombuses ◇ yellow.

Directions: Colour the star ☆ red.

Page 262

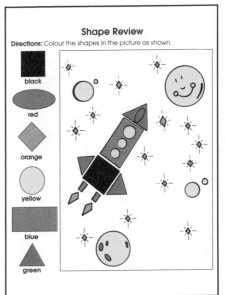

Shape Review

Directions: Colour the shapes in the picture as shown.

black

red

orange

yellow

blue

green

Page 263

Shape Review

Directions: Trace the circles
Trace the squares
Trace the rectangles
Trace the triangles
Trace the ovals
Trace the rhombuses

red
blue
yellow
green
purple
orange

Page 264

Classifying: Stars

Help Bob find the stars.

Directions: Colour all the stars blue.

How many stars did you and Bob find? __10__

Page 265

Classifying: Shapes

Mary and Rudy are taking a trip into space. Help them find the stars, moons, circles and rhombuses.

Directions: Colour the shapes.

Use yellow for ☆'s.   Use blue for ☾'s.
Use red for ○'s.   Use purple for ◇'s.

How many stars? __5__   How many moons? __5__
How many circles? __4__   How many rhombuses? __4__

Page 266

Classifying: Shapes

Directions: Look at the shapes. Answer the questions.

1. How many all-white shapes? __3__
2. How many all-blue shapes? __3__
3. How many half-white shapes? __3__
4. How many all-blue stars? __1__
5. How many all-white circles? __1__
6. How many half-blue shapes? __3__

Page 267

Same and Different: Shapes

Directions: Colour the shape that looks the same as the first shape in each row.

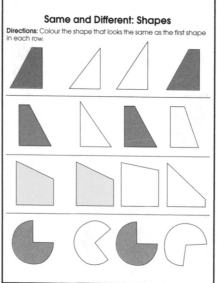

Page 268

Same and Different: Shapes

Directions: Draw an **X** on the shapes in each row that do not match the first shape.

Page 269

Copying: Shapes and Colours

Directions: Colour your circle to look the same.

Directions: Colour your square to look the same.

Directions: Trace the triangle. Colour it to look the same.

Directions: Trace the star. Colour it to look the same.

Page 270

Copying: Shapes and Colours

Directions: Colour the second shape the same as the first one. Then draw and colour the shape two more times.

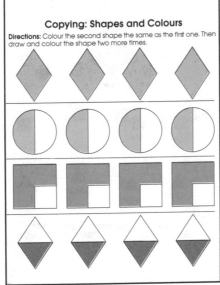

Page 271

Patterns: Shapes

Directions: Draw a line from the box on the left to the box on the right with the same shape and colour pattern.

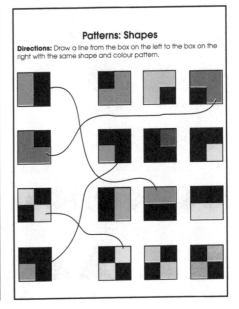

Page 272

Patterns: Shapes

Directions: Draw a line from the box on the left to the box on the right with the same shape and colour pattern.

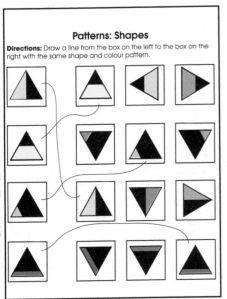

Page 273

Patterns: Find and Copy

Directions: Circle the shape in the middle box that matches the one on the left. Draw another shape with the same pattern in the box on the right.

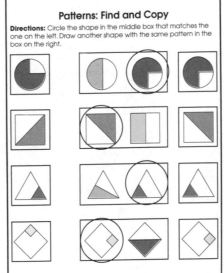

Page 274

Patterns

Directions: Draw what comes next in each pattern.

Example:

Page 275

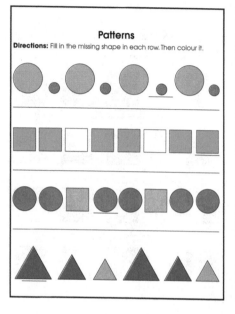

Patterns

Directions: Fill in the missing shape in each row. Then colour it.

Page 276

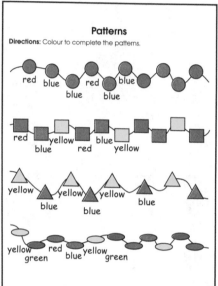

Patterns

Directions: Colour to complete the patterns.

red blue red blue
blue blue

red yellow blue
blue red yellow

yellow yellow yellow
blue blue blue

yellow red blue yellow
green blue green

Page 277

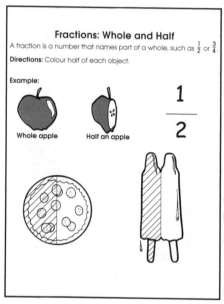

Fractions: Whole and Half

A fraction is a number that names part of a whole, such as $\frac{1}{2}$ or $\frac{3}{4}$.

Directions: Colour half of each object.

Example:

Whole apple   Half an apple

$\dfrac{1}{2}$

Page 278

Fractions: Halves $\frac{1}{2}$

$\dfrac{1}{2}$ $\dfrac{\text{Part shaded or divided}}{\text{Number of equal parts}}$

Directions: Colour only the shapes that show halves.

Page 279

Fractions: Thirds $\frac{1}{3}$

Directions: Circle the objects that have 3 equal parts.

Page 280

Fractions: Fourths $\frac{1}{4}$

Directions: Circle the objects that have four equal parts.

Page 281

Fractions: Thirds and Fourths

Directions: Each object has 3 equal parts. Colour one section.

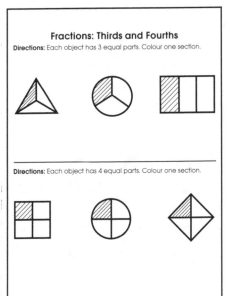

Directions: Each object has 4 equal parts. Colour one section.

Page 282

Review: Fractions

Directions: Count the equal parts, then write the fraction.

Example:

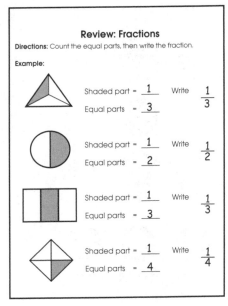

Shaded part = __1__   Write $\frac{1}{3}$
Equal parts = __3__

Shaded part = __1__   Write $\frac{1}{2}$
Equal parts = __2__

Shaded part = __1__   Write $\frac{1}{3}$
Equal parts = __3__

Shaded part = __1__   Write $\frac{1}{4}$
Equal parts = __4__

Page 283

Review

Directions: Write the missing numbers by counting by tens and fives.

__10__, 20, __30__, __40__, __50__, __60__, 70, __80__, __90__, 100

5, __10__, 15, __20__, __25__, 30, __35__, __40__, __45__, __50__

Directions: Colour the object with thirds red. Colour the object with halves blue. Colour the object with fourths green.

Directions: Draw a line to the correct equal part.

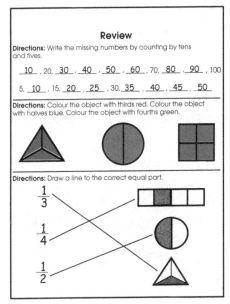

$\frac{1}{3}$

$\frac{1}{4}$

$\frac{1}{2}$

Page 284

Tracking: Straight Lines

Directions: Draw a straight line from A to B. Use a different colour crayon for each line.

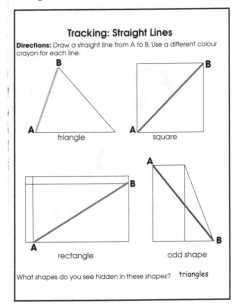

triangle   square

rectangle   odd shape

What shapes do you see hidden in these shapes?   triangles

Page 285

Tracking: Different Paths

Directions: Trace three paths from A to B.

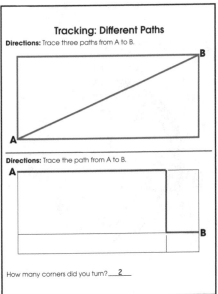

Directions: Trace the path from A to B.

How many corners did you turn? __2__

Page 286

Tracking: Different Paths

Help Megan find Mark.

Directions: Trace a path from Megan to Mark.

Paths may vary.

How many different paths can she follow to reach him? __8__

Page 287

Tracking: Different Paths

Directions: Use different colours to trace three paths the bear could take to get the honey.

Page 288

Time: Hour

The short hand of the clock tells the hour. The long hand tells how many minutes after the hour. When the minute hand is on the **12**, it is the beginning of the hour.

Directions: Look at each clock. Write the time.

Example:

_3_ o'clock

_9_ o'clock   _1_ o'clock   _8_ o'clock   _11_ o'clock

_5_ o'clock   _2_ o'clock   _10_ o'clock   _12_ o'clock

Page 289

Time: Hour, Half-Hour

The short hand of the clock tells the hour. The long hand tells how many minutes after the hour. When the minute hand is on the **6**, it is on the half-hour. A half-hour is thirty minutes. It is written **:30**, such as **5:30**.

Directions: Look at each clock. Write the time.

Example:

hour   half-hour
_1_ : _30_

_4_ : _30_   _5_ : _30_   _3_ : _30_   _8_ : _30_

_6_ : _30_   _2_ : _30_   _10_ : _30_   _9_ : _30_

Page 290

Time: Hour, Half-Hour

Directions: Draw the hands on each clock to show the correct time.

2:30   9:00

7:00   4:30

3:00   1:30

Page 291

Time: Counting by Fives

Directions: Fill in the numbers on the clock face. Count by fives around the clock.

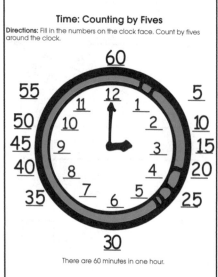

60

55   11   12   1   5

50   10   2   10

45   9   3   15

40   8   4   20

35   7   6   5   25

30

There are 60 minutes in one hour.

Page 292

Time: Review

Directions: Look at the time on the digital clocks and draw the hands on the clocks.

10:00   5:00

Directions: Look at each clock. Write the time.

_3_ o'clock   _2_ o'clock

Directions: Look at each clock. Write the time.

_1_ : _30_   _10_ : _30_   _4_ : _30_

Page 293

Review: Time

Directions: Tell what time it is on the clocks.

8:00

12:30

9:30

10:00

12:00

8:30

Page 294

Review: Time

Directions: Match the time on the clock with the digital time.

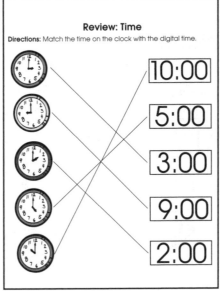

10:00

5:00

3:00

9:00

2:00

Page 295

Money: Penny and Nickel

A penny is worth one cent. It is written 1¢ or $.01. A nickel is worth five cents. It is written 5¢ or $.05.

Directions: Count the money and write the answers.

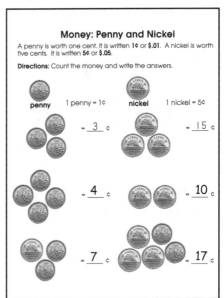

penny   1 penny = 1¢   nickel   1 nickel = 5¢

= __3__ ¢   = __15__ ¢

= __4__ ¢   = __10__ ¢

= __7__ ¢   = __17__ ¢

Page 296

Money: Penny, Nickel, Dime

A penny is worth one cent. It is written 1¢ or $.01. A nickel is worth five cents. It is written 5¢ or $.05. A dime is worth ten cents. It is written 10¢ or $.10.

Directions: Add the coins pictured and write the total amounts in the blanks.

Example:

dime   nickel   nickel   pennies
10¢ = 5¢ + 5¢ =   10¢

10¢ + 1¢ = __11__ ¢   10¢ + __5__ ¢ = __15__ ¢

10 ¢ + __5__ ¢+ __1__ ¢ =   __16__ ¢

10 ¢+ __3__ ¢ = __13__ ¢

Page 297

Money

Directions: Match the amounts in each purse to the price tags.

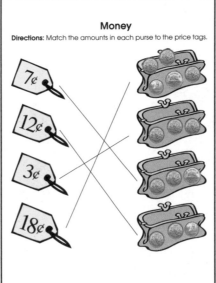

7¢

12¢

3¢

18¢

Page 298

Money: Penny, Nickel, Dime

Directions: Match the correct amount of money with the price of the object.

Page 299

Review: Money

Directions: What time is it?

_3_ o'clock

Directions: Draw the hands on each clock.

2:30   7:30   11:00

Directions: How much money?

= _22_ ¢   = _19_ ¢

Directions: Add or subtract.

9 + 3 = _12_   6 + 8 = _14_   15 - 9 = _6_

12 - 8 = _4_   12 + 2 = _14_   7 + 6 = _13_

Page 300

Review

Directions: Follow the instructions.
1. How much money?

_8_ ¢

2. 57 = Tens _5_   Ones _7_   128 = Hundreds _1_   Tens _2_   Ones _8_

3. What is this shape? Circle the answer.

(Square)
Triangle
Circle

What is this shape? __triangle__

4. Shaded part = _1_   Write $\frac{1}{2}$
   Equal parts = _2_

   Shaded part = _1_   Write $\frac{1}{4}$
   Equal parts = _4_

5. 12 + 3 = _15_   9 + 6 = _15_   15 - 7 = _8_

Page 301

Measurement

A ruler has 36 centimetres.

Directions: Cut out the ruler at the bottom of the page. Measure the objects to the nearest centimetres.

The screwdriver is _9_ centimetres long.

The pencil is _8_ centimetres long.

The pen is _6_ centimetres long.

The fork is _7_ centimetres long.